The Man with the Movie C

Art Center College

[

KINOfiles Film Companions
General Editor: Richard Taylor

Written for cineastes and students alike, KINOfiles are readable, authoritative, illustrated companion handbooks to the most important and interesting films to emerge from Russian cinema from its beginnings to the present. Each KINOfile investigates the production, context and reception of the film and the people who made it, and analyses the film itself and its place in Russian and World cinema. KINOfiles will also include films of the other countries that once formed part of the Soviet Union, as well as works by émigré film-makers working in the Russian tradition.

KINOfiles form a part of KINO: The Russian Cinema Series.

THE MAN WITH THE MOVIE CAMERA

GRAHAM ROBERTS

KINOfiles Film Companion 2

I.B.Tauris *Publishers*
LONDON • NEW YORK

Published in 2000 by I.B.Tauris & Co Ltd
Victoria House, Bloomsbury Square, London WC1B 4DZ
175 Fifth Avenue, New York NY 10010
www.ibtauris.com

In the United States of America and in Canada distributed by
St Martins Press, 175 Fifth Avenue, New York NY 10010

ISBN 1 86064 394 9

A full CIP record for this book is available from the British Library
A full CIP record for this book is available from the Library of Congress

Library of Congress catalog card: available

Typeset in Monotype Calisto by the Midlands Book Typesetting Company,
Loughborough, Leicestershire
Printed and bound in Great Britain by MPG Books Ltd, Bodmin, Cornwall

Contents

Illustrations

All the illustrations in this book come from the (BFI Films: Stills, Posters and Designs)

Acknowledgements

Thanks are due to:
Seth Feldman and Marina Goldovskaia for their encouragement. Nigel and Kve Humberstone and a host of students at the University of Leeds who stimulated me to look at *The Man with the Movie Camera* again and in different ways; Benjamin Sher, whose enthusiasm for all things Russian is so infectious and Chris Dashiel for his infectious love of Vertov's film.

Yuri Tsivian has been a source of (accurate) detail, as has Nikolai Izvolov. Richard Taylor was – as always – a splendid (and entertaining) editor. All at IB Tauris – especially Philippa Brewster and Gwenaëlle Fossard – aided me in my efforts with professionalism and sympathy.

I am especially grateful to everyone at the Institute of Communications Studies, University of Leeds. Particular credit goes to Professor Philip Taylor and the indefatigable Isobel Rich, whose patience and forbearance during the writing was beyond the call of duty.

I should like to express my gratitude to Heather Wallis who was asked for, and showed, more forbearance than anyone. Finally, thanks to Charlotte and Samuel who were responsible for many of the delays (and most of the sleepless nights) – this book is dedicated to them and the 'spinning gypsy': DZIGA VERTOV

Graham Roberts, May 2000

Note on Transliteration

Transliteration from the Cyrillic to the Latin alphabet is a perennial problem for writers on Russian subjects. I have opted for a dual system: in the text I have used the Library of Congress system (without diacritics), but I have broken from this system (a) when a Russian name has a clear English version (e.g. Maria instead of Mariia, Alexander instead of Aleksandr); (b) when a Russian name has an accepted English spelling, or when Russian names are of Germanic origin (e.g. Yeltsin instead of Eltsin; Eisenstein instead of Eizenshtein); (c) when a Russian surname ends in -ii or -yi this is replaced by a single -y (e.g. Trotsky instead of Trotstkii), and all Christian names end in a single -i. In the scholarly apparatus I have adhered to the Library of Congress system (with diacritics) for the specialist.

Production Details and Credits

Production: The All-Ukrainian Photo and Cinema Administration (VUFKU) – Kiev
Director ('Author-supervisor of the experiment'): Dziga Vertov
Chief cameraman: Mikhail Kaufman
Editor: Elizaveta Svilova

There was clearly a second camera unit working on this film, not least to film Kaufman. They remain uncredited. However, I would suggest that the *other* 'Man with the Movie Camera' was Peter Zotov.[1]

Format: b/w 35mm

Camera: Debrie with Zeiss lens (35 and 70mm)

Length: Ia. Makhlina *Repertuarnyi ukazatel' kinorepertuara* (Moscow, 1936), which Seth Feldman uses as his authoritative source, gives a length of 1889m. Both Feldman and I have seen archive prints of approximately 1830m. (which agrees with Leyda's figure in *Kino*). The timing of the film is obviously dependent upon the speed of projection. In general Western scholars have been working at 18 frames per second (whilst in Moscow I watched the film at 24fps). It has now become more usual to run the film at 24fps.[2] The British Film Institute video and DVD print – for which the film is run at 24fps – lasts 66 minutes, 30 seconds.

Release: Kiev – 8 January 1929;[3] The Hermitage Theatre in Moscow – 9 April 1929.

Vertov showed *The Man with the Movie Camera* on his trip to Europe in July 1929 (Berlin and Paris).

The film was made available throughout Europe via the Paris offices of Mezhrabpom.[4]

The film reached New York in the spring of 1930 where it had such a life-changing effect on Jay Leyda.[5]

Availability: For more than 60 years *The Man with the Movie Camera* was available only in archive prints. These prints were in various states of completeness and quality of preservation. For example the print held at the All-Union State Institute of Cinematography (VGIK) in Moscow was extraordinarily well-preserved but sections were missing and copied out of sequence. A complete and accurate print of the film was presented at the Teatro Verdi on 14 October 1995 as part of the Pordenone Silent Film Festival. The film was accompanied by music composed by the Alloy Orchestra based on Vertov's own notes.[6] This version of the film was produced for video by David Shepard and released by Kino International in the USA in 1995. A PAL-VHS version of this production is now available from the British Film Institute in the UK. This is the version (with time-code) that I have used for my own textual analysis.

Details of filming/editing

The filmed material compiled into *The Man with the Movie Camera* came from four sources:

1 Moscow: material filmed for *The Cine-Eye* [Kino-glaz] during 1924 and 1925: e.g. the 'magician and children' sequence and the famous sites of the capital including : Tverskaia Street, the Bolshoi Theatre and the square in front of it.
2 Kiev: material filmed throughout the preparation/montage period i.e. May–September 1928: e.g. the cinema, the train station.
3 Donbas: material gathered during the filming of *The Eleventh Year* [Odinnadtsatii] in the Spring of 1928.
4 Yalta and Odessa in the summer of 1928, e.g. the beach, the funfair, holiday camp and firing range as well as the 'Proletariat' cinema and the Workers' Club.

Editing and re-editing took place throughout the filming period. There were further re-edits after showings of a rough cut in Kiev during the last week of September 1928.

Notes

1. see p. 72.
2. The video runs at 25fps.
3. The Gosfilmofond booklet – *Dziga Vertov* (Moscow, 1967) p. 5 – suggests that the film was also shown in Moscow workers' clubs – with 'arguments and discussions' – before the official premiere.
4. Oswell Blakeston reviewed the film for *Close Up* ('Three Russian films', vol. V, no. 2 pp. 144–50) in August 1929, after seeing the film through the good offices of 'Mr. Carlovitch'. He concludes: 'The work of Vertoff (*sic*) is no longer legendary. We have seen it, others have seen it. Everybody must fight till they do see it.' This fight seems to have been largely unsuccessful.
5. J. Leyda *Kino* (London, 1987) p. 251.
6. These notes have been seen by Seth Feldman in Vertov's personal archive in Moscow, and were retrieved and utilized by Paolo Cherchi Usai of George Eastman House.

Preface

Dziga Vertov's *The Man with the Movie Camera* [Chelovek s kinoapparatom, 1929] is a remarkable film. It is unlike anything that came before or after it in Vertov's *oeuvre*, Soviet cinema or indeed the history of film. The film is a documentary made by one of the most prolific and vociferous defenders of non-fiction (or 'unplayed') film. 'Unplayed film' (*neigrovaia fil'ma*) was the contemporary Soviet term for the genre. I have chosen – whenever possible – to use the term 'unplayed' as opposed to 'non-fiction' or 'documentary' in an effort to highlight Vertov's approach to *using* factual material. Thus it is the difference *in the material itself* from scripted drama that is important. (Vertov's own phrase was 'life caught unawares' (zhizn' vrasplokh)). Vertov saw documentaries as the *only* valid form of film. *The Man with the Movie Camera* is a statement of commitment to the documentary approach. It is also a 'box of tricks' which serves as an essential example of Soviet montage and a catalogue of the possibilities of filming technique.

Vertov and his wife and editor Elizaveta Svilova constructed the film from material 'captured' by the 'Cine-Eye' team during the turbulent years 1924–28. It is a document of a period of transition in the history of the Soviet Union, of modernism and Constructivism – indeed of the cinema itself.

The Man with the Movie Camera was previewed by the Ukrainian Photo and Cinema Administration [VUFKU] in the autumn of 1928. It had its first public showings in Kiev on 8 January and Moscow on 9 April 1929. The film was then quickly shelved in the Soviet Union whilst going on to some critical success (or at least interest) after screenings in Berlin,

Paris and London. It stands as one of the most important films in the history of documentary cinema. It is also a creative masterpiece.

The primary aim of this book is to explain how such a film came to be made in the Soviet Union in 1927–28. In doing so, I will reposition Vertov as a political film-maker and his master-piece as a political film (however flawed or unsuccessful in its propagandistic role). Film historians such as Michelson[1] and Petrić[2] have positioned Vertov as an influential part of the European modernist avant-garde. The argument central to this book and my reading of the film is that it is both historically more accurate and indeed more interesting to see Vertov as a film-maker committed to a political position (Marxism-Leninism) and to a rigorously thought-out documentary practice. As part of this more overtly political positioning I will also return often to Michelson's comment on Vertov's failure to please his political masters that: 'he had instead become cinema's Trotsky.'[3] I would contend that Vertov saw himself more as the cinema's 'man of Steel' (Stalin). I will argue that *The Man with the Movie Camera* can be viewed as a cinematic affirmation of the Stalinist policies about to unfold: crush resistance in the countryside, urbanize, industrialize, purge opposition.

This study has begun with a presentation of the key facts and figures about the film: dates, places and circumstances of filming and exhibition. A synopsis of *The Man with the Movie Camera* (along with a discussion of the concept of 'plot' in relation to the film) follows and, after it, a look at the context of the film in terms of Vertov's previous work and his theoretical writing and manifestos. The study concludes with an explanation of Vertov's position in the Soviet film industry in the mid- to late 1920s and a discussion of the political circumstances of the Soviet Union 1921–1929 to contextualize the film further.

The analysis of the film itself consists of a close textual reading of *The Man with the Movie Camera* which seeks at all times to relate each shot, sequence of shots and overall structure to Vertov's stated aim to 'capture life unawares'. This capturing process will be analysed with reference to Vertov's commitment to engage in the 'communist decoding of reality'.[4]

The film is approached as series of sequences and in a sectional/structural manner. My aim has been to show how the film can work for a first-time viewer. I absolutely agree with those critics, e.g. Vlada Petrić and Yuri Tsivian, who argue that the film needs to be seen over and over again but this loses the shock of immediacy that is so essential. I have tried to guide viewers and give them a sense of the film's architecture. I hope that they may then wish to argue with my sectioning, views on individual shots and sequences and the conclusions I draw on the film as a whole. *The Man with the Movie Camera* is a very rich text that can stand such close attention and debate.

In the light of this clear statement of support for the film I also feel the need to explain why the film was seen as a failure and how this perceived failure affected Vertov's career for the rest of his creative life. This account extends to an insight not only into the workings of Soviet cinema but also into the nature of the Soviet system itself.

The study concludes with an analysis of the film's (and Vertov's) reputation in the ensuing decades. This section includes a review of the historiography of Vertov, a discussion of his continuing influence and some more recent reactions from Annette Michelson, Vlada Petrić, Seth Feldman and others.

Notes

1. In her introduction to Kevin O'Brien's translations of Vertov's written output: *Kino-Eye: the Writings of Dziga Vertov,* Berkeley, 1984.
2. V. Petrić *Constructivism in Film*, Cambridge, 1987.
3. *Kino Eye* p. lxi.
4. 'The Birth of Kino-Eye', *Kino-Eye*, p. 42.

1. Plot and Synopsis

To talk about 'plot' with reference to a non-fiction film, particularly this most militant of non-fiction films, may seem perverse. However, in general terms non-fiction film does require a narrative role/structure.[1] Early documentary makers, e.g. Robert Flaherty, were attracted to the classic genre of the journey,[2] not least as a tool for spectator engagement. Winston astutely points out that this strategy: 'solved actuality's big narrative problem – closure.'[3] The other favoured structure, particularly when attempting to present the chaotic activity of the city was 'a day in the life'. The most famous example of this approach is Walter Ruttman's *Berlin: Symphony of a Great City* [Berlin: die Sinfonie der Großstadt, Germany, 1927]. Among the many concepts and conventions that Vertov plays with in his film is the diurnal narrative and indeed narrative itself.

The Man with the Movie Camera does have a plot. It is typical of the playful nature of the film that it initially appears to be structured around a (generic) 'day in the life' format. In this case we appear to be watching the cameraman's day as it connects with a (constructed) city. The breaks from this narrative are largely cutaways to show the process of the energy production that makes all the activity possible. The film continually pulls the viewer away from the possibility of too simplistic a reading. Most obviously, the diegesis is clearly constructed from footage from several sites. Not only is there a lack of geographical continuity but temporal continuity is also broken deliberately and ostentatiously. Sequences, or more usually fragments of sequences, are repeated and utilized in different juxtapositions.

One third of the way into the movie the narrative is halted as the film itself 'stops' for an educative exercise in editing technique. From that point on the 'day in the life' reading becomes increasingly difficult.

All human life is here from birth to death via childhood, marriage, divorce, work, rest and play. The last three activities are a key to Vertov's message. The overall structure of the film does lend itself to the more ideological view of the 'day' as one-third rest, one-third work, one-third (constructive) leisure.[4]

The audience will always be looking to make sense of the visual material they are presented with. Invariably this will be predicated upon the desire to find a narrative thread. If we take the position of an unprepared viewer trying to ascertain – and indeed programmed to expect – a 'story' from any movie, it is possible to watch *The Man with the Movie Camera* as a narrative (if a rather unusual and disjointed one).

Synopsis

The moving images begin with a cameraman 'mounting' a giant camera to survey 'the city'. The 'man with the movie camera' (i.e. the cameraman) enters a cinema that is being prepared to show the film *The Man with the Movie Camera*. The audience enters, the band wait and then begin to accompany the film.

A woman is dreaming of the city (still asleep). Various scenes of inactivity (including sleeping cab drivers and babies) illustrate this. Machinery stands idle. A car arrives at an apartment block to pick up the cameraman. He films an onrushing train and appears to be caught on the track. The woman awakes, dresses and washes. The city begins to awake. A vagrant stirs and laughs at the camera. On Tverskaia Street in Moscow, previously deserted, people appear.

The cameraman begins his tour through the city that is now bustling. Meanwhile miners work to dig the coal that fuels the activity of the factories that spring into action. The machinery, which had previously been still, is now working. The cameraman films a street market and various means of transport including buses, trams and aeroplanes. He strides through the crowds. He observes the opening of shops and the activity of a policeman on traffic duty. At the main railway station in Kiev cabs await passengers. The cameraman pursues them, filming groups of passengers. Their images, and others including laughing children, are frozen – and brought to life – by the film editor in her laboratory.

Activity in the city continues: people marry and divorce; a funeral takes place and a birth. The pace of life speeds up. A woman's eye (that of the editor) blinks and surveys the skyline. Her gaze swoops down on the streets. An accident has occurred and the cameraman follows the ambulance to the site. Then he films a fire engine on an emergency call.

The editor cuts together the activities of a beauty parlour and manual labour. Whilst she edits, other women sew. Machine operators become like machines. Miners continue to quarry. The activity becomes more and more frenetic until the machines come to a halt. The workers wash and change. Workers engage in healthy activities on the beach. A magician entertains children and the camera does magic tricks of appearance and disappearance too.

The cameraman films the production of a wall newspaper and is drawn to an item about sport. The fit and happy Soviet workers engage in exercise. The cameraman takes his equipment for a swim.

The cameraman enters a bar. The camera becomes drunk. It staggers past a 'Candles and Icons' store. No Soviet audience would fail to understand the message that religion and intoxication are closely linked. As an antidote, 'the man with the movie camera' marches purposefully to the Lenin Workers' Club (in Odessa). Workers read, play chess and listen to the radio. A musical performance utilizing household items takes place on screen.

Back in the cinema the audience is watching as the camera, much to their amusement, takes on a life of its own. They also enjoy a montage of dancing and music making. Crowds mass on screen as the audience looks on. Giant cameras dominate the city as the Bolshoi Theatre implodes. Time speeds up. Images from earlier in the film return with increasing rapidity. The pace continues into a blur until the camera closes its 'eye'.

This torrent of action and cinematographic magic would be enough – if not too much – for any audience. But there is more to *The Man with the Movie Camera* than meets the (unsuspecting) eye – much more. How much more will be explained in the next two chapters, which will contextualize the film and analyse its 'text'.

Notes

1   Or, as Brian Winston titled a chapter in his seminal work *Claiming the Real* (London, 1995): 'Non-Narrative: Works Better in the Head than on the Screen'.

2 Flaherty worked in this way on the MacKenzie expedition footage that he
   shot in 1914–15 and which laid the groundwork for *Nanook of the North*
   (1922). *Nanook* includes two journey sequences: the fishing trip and the
   walrus hunt. Film-makers before Flaherty had used the journey *to* (rather
   than *of* their subject: e.g. Edward Sheriff Curtis's *In the Land of the Headhun-
   ters* (1914).
3 Winston p. 104.
4 see L. Trotskii, 'Vodka, the Church and the Cinema', *Pravda*, 12 July 1923,
   translation in R. Taylor and I. Christie eds., *The Film Factory* (London,
   1988) pp. 94–7.

2. The Historical Context

'My path leads to the creation of a fresh perception of the world. I decipher in a new way a world unknown to you.'

Dziga Vertov, 'Cine-Eyes – a Revolution', 1923[1]

'The cinema is the greatest means of mass agitation. The task is to take it into our hands.'

Stalin to the 13th Party Congress, May 1924[2]

The Man with the Movie Camera cannot be understood – indeed made much sense of – without knowledge of its position in the specific historical circumstances and longer term context of its filming and release and Vertov's relationship with Soviet cinema up to the point of its making. This chapter will contextualize the film within Vertov's preceding career and the developments within Soviet cinema up to and including the period of the making of *The Man with the Movie Camera*. However, as a political film made by a political film-maker it is absolutely necessary to begin contextualization with an overview of the general political background.

Vertov's first independent documentary *The Cine-Eye* was released in October 1924. In other words, the film emerged at the mid-point of the New Economic Policy (NEP) launched by Lenin at the 10th Party Congress in March 1921. By the time of the Party Congress the Civil War, which had threatened to end the Bolshevik regime in 1918–19, was practically won. However, as external threat retreated, internal problems rose to crisis point. Peasants rioted against grain requisitioning in the Don region. Workers struck for more control in Petrograd. The Kronstadt garrison, cradle of the 1917 Revolution, was gripped by mutiny. Resistance was crushed as the Congress met but

Lenin was aware that the economic roots of the dissent needed to be dealt with if the Bolshevik state was to survive. His 'New Economic Policy' of a limited return to the market in agriculture and light industry was accepted, but resented, by the delegates.

The other, and in the long term more profound, change which occurred at the 10th Party Congress was the banning of factions.[3] This centralizing disciplinary measure was necessitated by a need to confirm Party discipline at time when the Bolsheviks were a very small minority in the country they proposed to lead towards socialism. It was the first serious step towards the rigid centralization and intolerance of any debate about, never mind deviation from, the 'Party line' (by which was meant, ultimately, the leader's opinions) on all forms of activity.

The logical conclusion of this tendency came in the years of 'High Stalinism' after the Second World War but could be seen reaching absurd – not to say obscene – heights by the 1930s. In April 1922, at the 11th Party Congress, Stalin was made General Secretary of the Party. He could begin building his system of patronage which would leave him in a position of unassailable power by the time of *The Man with the Movie Camera*.

During 1923 the Soviet Union, so named in December 1922, took on an air of confidence and longevity. The 12th Party Congress had met and confirmed its disciplined leadership of the state (Lenin's concerns about chauvinist national policy and a building of rigid hierarchy were successfully hidden by Trotsky and Stalin). A new constitution was being drafted. However, the economy was in severe danger of collapse. In what became known as the 'scissors crisis', the rise in the price of industrial goods far outstripped agricultural prices. The result was that the peasants had no reason to produce a surplus and thus there was no 'surplus value' to fuel economic growth (or indeed to feed the growing urban population. A compromise with the peasants was allowed once again (but for the final time). To the Party cadres the issue was a political one – was the New *Economic* Policy really 'The New *Exploitation* of the Proletariat'?

The fundamental weakness of the Soviet economy – and with it the NEP – was revealed, at least to the leadership. Lenin was increasingly ill, having suffered strokes in May 1922 and March 1923. When he died in January 1924, Lenin left major questions over the future development of the Soviet Union and of his succession unanswered. His acolytes squabbled amongst themselves on matters of policy which

1. Split screen experiment from *Forward Soviet* (1926)

must also be seen as tools in a struggle for power. As Vertov 'caught life unawares' between *The Cine-Eye* and *The Man with the Movie Camera*, Stalin was able to catch his opponents – Trotsky, Zinoviev, Kamenev and later Bukharin – unawares and attain the supreme power that enabled him to transform the Soviet Union into a new Russian Empire.

The year 1924 was one of relative economic success and a more stable international situation. Sun Yat-Sen's Nationalist Kuomintang movement in China had assiduously formed links with the communists and had gone as far as to recognize the government of the Soviet Union and to invite Soviet military advisers in June. Great Britain had become the first Western power to recognize the Soviet Union and had established diplomatic links in February of the same year. By the end of 1924 the British Labour government had fallen – over the 'Red Scare' of the entirely fictitious 'Zinoviev letter' – leading to renewed fears of aggressive powers in the West. Warlord risings in China had raised the fear of instability in the East.

The Party rank and file already knew that the Soviet Union was in constant danger. The Party leadership knew only too well that the Union was not even strong (or united) enough to defend itself from concerted attack never mind to pursue energetically the cause of international revolution. This international strategy, one which Lenin had firmly believed would secure Soviet power in the long run, no longer seemed realistic. All attempts to follow the Bolshevik lead, including risings in Germany and Hungary, had failed.

At the end of 1924 Stalin was ready to use 'the concrete situation' to attack what he chose to call: 'Trotsky's theory of permanent revolution' in the Party press. The General Secretary felt able to put forward the opinion that it was possible – even a moral imperative – to achieve 'Socialism in one country'. Thus, in April 1925, the 14th Party Congress, dominated by Stalin's new cadres, could resolve that: 'in general the victory of socialism is unconditionally possible in one country.'[4]

The change in policy was a political victory for Stalin over Trotsky, who had already been persuaded to resign his power base as Commissar for War in January 1925. It also confirmed Stalin's perspicacity in offering, in order to reach a trade agreement with Japan, to restrict the subversive activities of the Moscow-based Third International. Developments during the run up to the Congress confirmed the need for the Soviet Union to look to its own resources. On 27 February Hitler was released from prison to be greeted as a national figure by a crowd of 4000. The day after, Ebert died, to be replaced as German President by the ultra-conservative nationalist Hindenburg. On 12 March Sun Yat-Sen died. His successor Chiang Kai Shek was keen to show his anti-communist credentials by expelling the Soviet adviser Borodin.

The crucial result of the change to a doctrine of 'socialism in one country', and the political doctrine that had to be represented in documentary films, was the need to reassess the nature of economic development in the Soviet Union.[5] Having abandoned the chimera of imminent world revolution, the leaders of the Soviet Union had to focus on quickening industrialization without outside help.

Stalin's opponents on the left saw a solution in an adaptation of Marx's 'primitive capitalist accumulation' to 'primitive socialist accumulation'. Basically the State would seize control of the whole economy and divert all resources to industrial development. The NEP would be over. As Hosking put it:

2. Mikhail Kaufman: 'the man with the movie camera'

> The Oppositionists were moved by a dislike of NEP which was
> widely shared by the party. They were repelled by the raucous,
> untidy, money-grabbing peasant markets, by the debauchery of the
> night-clubs ...[6]

This is a position which could be read from Vertov's *Cine-Eye* and
Forward Soviet! [Shagai, Sovet! 1926]. More subtle economists,
including Bukharin, argued that the crisis of isolation could hardly be
improved by engendering a massive economic disruption at home.
Better to encourage the steady growth in the economy as a whole and
attempt to socialize the countryside and light industry by the growth of
cooperatives. For the time being Stalin chose to agree. This was the
position, admittedly expressed very aggressively, put forward in *One
Sixth of the World* [Shestaia chast' mira, 1926].

When Vertov left Moscow for the Ukraine in February 1927 the

Soviet Union was once again about to enter a period of deep crisis. As during the Civil War, the Bolsheviks' propensity now to take action quickly and ruthlessly, especially when defending their own position, was thrown into sharp relief.

In domestic politics the Party continued to splinter at the top. Zinoviev and Kamenev had moved into opposition in fear of Stalin's power. Opposition from the old leaders meant little to Stalin as he now had a firm grip on the rank and file through the patronage of 'Lenin enrolments' which had increased Party membership in 1924. Nonetheless, the sight of the men who led the Revolution engaged in bitter policy disputes led to an increasing feeling of crisis.

Trotsky, Kamenev and Zinoviev managed to cobble together an alliance with other 'factions'. In July 1926 Kamenev was expelled from the Politburo. In October Trotsky and Zinoviev followed. Their attempts to bring Stalin down, or at least to heel, simply exacerbated the dire weakness of their own position.

A major bone of contention between Stalin and Trotsky had been the former's appeasing attitude to the Chinese nationalists. That policy began to be exposed very badly. After major victories in early 1927, the nationalists split with communists on 24 March and initiated the slaughter of the communists in Shanghai on 12 April. Trotsky and Zinoviev had used the news of Chiang Kai Shek's coup against his erstwhile allies as a reason to attack Stalin – who had personally engineered an alliance with the Chinese Nationalist leader.[7] Stalin's in-built majority, by then at all levels of the Party, meant his position was unassailable. The opposition's talking up of 'the crisis', for example Trotsky related that 'the Soviet government was hanging by a thread',[8] played into Stalin's hands.

In Europe the forces of anti-communism seemed to be gaining strength. In May 1927 the Nazis attempted to seize power in Austria. In Britain the Conservatives were firmly in power and, after the debacle of the General Strike, organized labour was on the retreat. A break in Anglo-Soviet diplomatic relations in May led to a 'war scare' which coloured the nature of the celebrations for the tenth anniversary of the October Revolution.

During what should have been a moment of triumph the Communist Party was experiencing what turned out to be the last serious internal struggle for 30 years. On 27 December 1927 the 15th Party Congress expelled Trotsky from the Party and banished him to

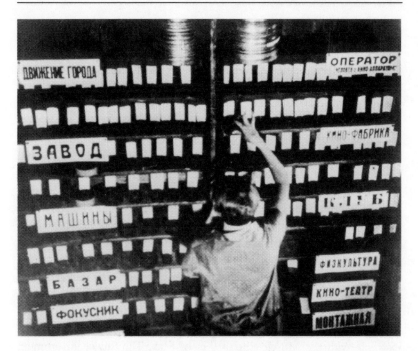

3. Svilova at work

Turkmenistan. The same Congress resolved to collectivize Soviet agriculture and accelerate growth in the industrial sector. These decisions, taken in haste, fundamentally changed the role of the state and its relationship to its own citizens. 'Exploitation' was, after all, the only valid methodology at a time of crisis. The party rank and file were happy to agree.

From the autumn of 1927 the Stalinist conception of what constituted the Soviet Union had triumphed and would remain the model for development with little variation until the Gorbachev experiment of the 1980s. Vertov's films from the late 1920s confirm a belief in the Stalinist orthodoxy: always strengthen, always act politically and do so informed by an unyielding materialist realism.

At the start of 1928 Vertov edited together that celebration of Soviet might *The Eleventh Year* and Bliokh worked on the warning that was *Shanghai Document*. Further crises occurred which confirmed the need for rapid strengthening of Soviet industrial power, not least to increase its military capability. On 19 April the Japanese occupied Shantung province in Northern China. This was an area where the Soviet Union had economic interests in the railways. The Soviet Far East was also threatened. It was after all only five years since Japanese troops had been ejected from Vladivostok. On 8 June 1928 Chiang's troops entered Peking.

At home there was a further grain procurement crisis. In March 1928 the State Security Organization (OGPU) had uncovered an apparent conspiracy (by non-communist technicians) to undermine industrial development in the Donets Basin at a town called Shakhty. The Shakhty trial, which signalled the beginning of a campaign against 'wreckers' within the Soviet Union, opened in May. The citizens of the Soviet Union were about to be convinced that they lived in a beacon of socialism that was threatened on all sides and undermined from within.

The powers of the West seemed only too happy to add evidence. On 15 June 1928 US presidential candidate Hoover announced at the Republican Party convention in Kansas: 'We in America today are nearer to the triumph over poverty than ever before.' The US federal government increased its involvement in hydro-electric power, for example with the Muscle Shoals Act of May. The Soviet government could not show itself to be *less* active in the modernizing and empowering of its economy.

On 25 July the US signed a treaty with the Chinese Nationalists. On 6 October Chiang Kai Shek formally repudiated the communists. Alliances were building everywhere and they all appeared to be anti-communist. The negotiations for the Kellogg-Briand Pact could have been seen, from Moscow, as a peacekeeping conspiracy among the great imperialist powers.

It is essential to note that when *The Man with the Movie Camera* was made and released the economic crisis of capitalism had not occurred. The Soviet Union appeared to be losing the international class war. During the final editing of *The Man with the Movie Camera* the First Five-Year Plan was announced. In November Stalin explained the decision to the Central Committee of the Party:

We have caught up and overhauled the capitalist countries in our political forms. But that is not enough. To achieve the final victory of socialism in one country we also need to catch up and overhaul those countries in the technical and economic sense. Either we do it, or we shall be crushed.[9]

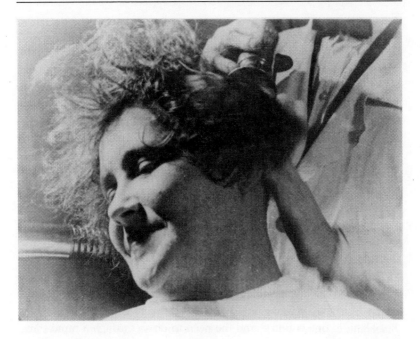

4. NEP-woman

As the film was released in the Ukraine, Trotsky was about to be expelled from the Soviet Union (31 January 1929). In February 1929 the Soviet Union signed the Litvinov Protocol with Poland and the Baltic states which seemed to confirm the non-expansionist spirit of 'Socialism in one country'. The commitment to the rapid strengthening of the Soviet Union was confirmed by the acceptance of the First Five-Year Plan by the 16th Party Congress in April 1929. The Plan was already in place anyway but the Congress voted to achieve its targets in four years. The need for urgency was fully confirmed by events abroad.

The concrete reality of the threat Stalin had warned them about could be seen in the aggressive acts of the 'imperialists', e.g. on 13 February 1929 the US Congress had passed the Cruiser Act (to build 15 cruisers and an aircraft carrier). This move could clearly be read in Moscow as the beginnings of preparations for war. In June came the news of the Young Plan, a US-sponsored attempt to solve the German reparations problem but which was also clearly an attempt to engineer a *rapprochement* between the Western powers, the very thing the Soviet Union did not want.

On 24 October 1929 'Black Wednesday' came and, as the 'Capitalist world' plunged into depression, the Soviet Union got its chance to crow. However, if the capitalist countries were about to face economic Armageddon, there was every reason to assume that this would make them more aggressive. Lenin's own work *On Imperialism* had made that very point.[10] The 'need for speed' was not averted it was even more certainly necessary. On 17 October Bukharin, the last hope of those who still believed in economic development at a realistic rate, had been expelled from the Politburo. By the time of Stalin's fiftieth birthday in December, which all forms of media in the Soviet Union celebrated fulsomely and vociferously, his position as undisputed leader was assured.

The Man with the Movie Camera is the product of the state of crisis which led to the abandonment of the NEP and the reassertion of more clearly Bolshevik policies. Vertov endorsed the policies of strengthening 'Socialism in one country' and the need to do so through a rapid transformation of the economy. That is why labour, the production of steel and coal, and the increased productive capacity of machines is so extensively explored.[11] The vestiges of the old (NEP) are fully explored in all their sordidness and a new world is constructed from the brightest and best elements of three different cities.

The film also exemplifies the belief that all things were possible in economic and social transformation. The film, like the campaigns for collectivization and crash industrialization, was the result of a belief that it is possible to engineer a fundamental reorganization of the facts of life. Vertov's manifesto (in print at the beginning of the film and in the visual diegesis) is an end to compromise. Vertov's whole professional career leading up to the making of the film can be seen as a struggle against any form of compromise.

Dziga Vertov was born in Belostock (now Białystok) on the western edge of the tsarist empire. His date of birth is usually given as 2 January 1896,[12] a week after the Lumières premiered their system for projecting moving pictures. He spent his early years as Denis Abramovich Kaufman, the bookish son of Jewish librarians. At some stage, possibly when he entered the Conservatoire, he Russified his patronymic to Arkadievich.[13] Whilst at the Conservatoire he moved away from literary efforts (he had written several fantasy novels)[14] and began experiments with arranging sounds. He also became interested in the psychology of perception.

In 1915 the Kaufman family fled the advancing German army and decamped to Petrograd. In the capital Denis furthered his scientific interests at the Psychoneurological Institute. He found himself increasingly attracted to avant-garde café society. In a Futurist gesture he began to call himself 'Dziga Vertov'. It is typical of Vertov that he should choose a name (a) because he liked the sound it made (possibly because it reminded him of film passing through a projector), and (b) because it contained a host of linguistic references and connections: 'Dziga' was the name of a spinning top as well as the Ukrainian term for a gypsy, 'Vertov' is derived from the Russian verb 'to spin'. He changed his name officially when he registered with the new Soviet authorities in the spring of 1918.

Vertov, the newly named Futurist artist, began constructing his 'laboratory of sound' in the winter of 1916–17. He recorded wild tracks of noises from the street onto wax discs. He then tried to edit them together with sounds created in his 'studio' into compositions. The equipment failed him. Acquaintances in the Petrograd cafés included film-makers such as newsreel cameraman Alexander Lemberg and the teenage designer Lev Kuleshov. They suggested that film would be a much more reliable medium. In 1924 Vertov was rather more poetic in his description of his epiphany:

> one day in the spring of 1918,[15] I was returning from the railway station. In my ears, there remained the chugs and bursts of steam from a departing train ... someone swearing ... a kiss ... somebody's exclamation ... laughter, a whistle, voices, the ringing of the station bell, the puffing of a locomotive ... whispers, shouts, farewells.[16]

This scene was recreated in the Kiev Central Station interlude in *The Man with the Movie Camera* (from 19 mins 50 seconds to 20 mins 50 seconds on the BFI version – this episode segues into the 'car chase').

Vertov continues:

> There is a need to find a machine not only to describe, but to register, to photograph these sounds ... Perhaps a camera ...

5. Woman as industrial icon

In January or February 1918 Mikhail Koltsov, chief of the Moscow Cinema Committee, offered Vertov a job administering the first Soviet newsreel *Kinonedelia* [Cine-week]. In the feverish atmosphere of Revolutionary Moscow Vertov battled to keep track of the scraps of newsreel footage arriving from the several fronts of the Civil War. Vertov learnt how to make films not in the studio or by studying the works of pre-Revolutionary or foreign 'masters'; but by dealing with the practical exigencies of constructing coherent newsreels out of disparate material under pressure of time and material deprivation. Every image, every scrap of film had to be used and reused to maximum effect.

Vertov's relationship to another, at that time much more experienced, young film-maker employed by the Committee is open to debate. Lev Kuleshov claimed later that he taught Vertov.[17] Both young men were certainly involved in a competition of innovation. Kuleshov conducted his 'Mosjoukine experiment' cutting unrelated images to create emotional effects (and laying claim to be the founder of montage theory). Vertov threw himself from a balcony of the Committee offices instructing the cameraman to over-crank the camera. The result was a slow motion study of a man striding, vacillating and jumping. It was also Vertov's first attempt to utilize the cinema's ability to decode and investigate 'life as it is'.

In July 1918 Koltsov was sent to the front, as were many of his best technicians. Thus Vertov found himself running the Moscow Cinema Committee. He set to work editing *Cine-Week*. By July 1919 production stopped due to lack of positive stock to make prints for distribution. Vertov needed to work. He re-edited the newsreel footage into a compilation documentary *The Anniversary of the Revolution* [Godovshchina Revoliutsii, 1919]. He then went to the front himself to film *The Battle for Tsaritsyn* [Boi pod Tsaritsynom, 1919]; during the editing of this material he worked with the most experienced editor in the Moscow offices, Elizaveta Svilova. They married in 1923. Svilova would edit every full-length film that Vertov ever finished.

Vertov spent 1920 organizing the filming and exhibiting of films on the propaganda train 'October Revolution'. The first agit-train, naturally named 'V. I. Lenin', had been dispatched to give ideological guidance to the troops fighting to regain the Kazan area from the rampaging Czech Legion. These trains usually contained a printing plant and a theatre group. Soon filmed material from the trains was being shown in Moscow and then circulated to the growing network of 'agit-stations' (*agitpunkty*) and on to the trains and boats built to bring revolutionary enlightenment, education and motivation to those areas still held by the Reds. The experience of the first train inspired Trotsky to order five similar 'literary instruction' trains. The aim of these trains was direct agitation on the move.

The Civil War experience had convinced Vertov that the future of cinema – particularly as a propaganda medium – was to be in non-fiction:

I was the manager of the cinema carriage on one of the agit-trains. ... The viewers were illiterate or semi-illiterate peasants. They could not read the subtitles. ... These unspoiled viewers could not understand the theatrical conventions.'[18]

In 1921 with the Civil War reaching a victorious conclusion Vertov returned to Petrograd to edit a 13-reel compilation of post-Revolutionary newsreels which was shown at the Third Congress of the Communist International. After this achievement Vertov could not simply return to editing newsreel. He was working at stretching the possibilities of the form with a carefully selected team of enthusiasts: Svilova, Ivan Beliakov and Alexander Lemberg were already collaborators. They were joined by Boris Frantsisson, Ilia Kopalin, Peter Zotov and – in 1922 – his newly demobbed brother Mikhail Kaufman.[19]

Kaufman, who had learnt his trade as a stills cameraman in the military, joined his brother and future sister-in-law as the prime movers in Vertov's team. Vertov's family called themselves 'The Council of Three'. They dubbed their group 'Cine-Eyes' (in Russian the neologism *Kinoki* conflates *kino* (cinema) with *oki* (eyes) whilst suggesting *okno* (window) and *okolo* (around)). It is typical of Vertov's approach that his choice of group name should be as full of connotations and descriptions of aims and methodology as his own pseudonym.

In the summer of 1922 the Cine-Eyes began to issue their *Cine-Truth* (Kinopravda) films. Vertov's title was, as usual, rich in connotations. The series of films were intended not only to show the world 'as it is' but also – by its reference to the Bolshevik Party's daily newspaper – aimed at the 'communist decoding of reality'. 'The Council of Three' went into print to publicize their militant views with 'We' in the magazine *Kino-Fot* in August 1922. As an opening shot it was impressive. As a statement of intent it gives a very accurate picture of what Vertov was trying to accomplish and what he did finally achieve in *The Man with the Movie Camera*.

WE proclaim the old films, based on the romance, theatrical films and the like,
to be leprous.
Keep away from them!
Keep your eyes off them!

... WE invite you:
to flee
the sweet embraces of romance,
the poison of the psychological novel
the clutches of the theatre of adultery;
to turn your backs on music,
to flee
out into the open, into four dimensions (three plus time), in search of our own material

... Hurrah for dynamic geometry, the race of points, lines, planes volumes.

Hurrah for the poetry of machines, propelled and driving; the poetry of levers, wheels and wings of steel; the iron cry of movements, the blinding grimaces of red-hot streams.[20]

During 1922 the *Cine-Truth* films became increasingly focused around a single theme. They were also produced less and less regularly. In 1923 there were just three. Vertov had other tasks to perform. He was working full-time on the State Film Company [Goskino] newsreel *Goskinokalendar* producing 53 editions between May 1923 and April 1925. In addition to an energetic campaign of speeches and letters proselytising the Cine-Eye method, Vertov was also feverishly drafting theoretical formulations of his methods. Most of these remained unpublished until Drobashenko's collection of Vertov's written output in 1966.[21]

In June 1923 Vertov did get his ideas into print through the pages of *Lef*, a journal edited by his friend Vladimir Mayakovsky. In 'The Cine-Eyes – a Revolution' we have perhaps the fullest statement of Vertov's most militant views. The early passages of the piece are repetitions of 'Council of Three' attacks on the validity of fiction film followed by a resolution (dated 10 April) which bemoans the lack of activity. The section entitled 'The Council of Three' is more enlightening on Vertov's approach to his own film-making:

Until now we have violated the movie camera and forced it to copy the work of our eye. The better the copy, the better the shooting was thought to be. Starting today we are liberating the camera and making it work in the opposite direction – away from copying.

The weakness of the human eye is manifest. We affirm the Cine-Eye, discovering the chaos of movement: the result of Cine-Eye's own movement; we affirm the Cine-Eye with its own dimensions of time and space, growing in strength and potential to the point of self-affirmation.[22]

A passage from section three of 'The Cine-Eyes. A Revolution' could be read as a preliminary sketch for *The Man with the Movie Camera* (indeed some of the images are contained in the film):

6. Children at the magic show

I am the Cine-Eye. I am a mechanical eye. I, a machine, show you the world only as I can see it.

Now and forever I free myself from human immobility. I am in constant motion.

I draw near, then away from objects. I crawl under. I crawl on top. I move apace with a galloping horse. I plunge full speed into a crowd ... manoeuvring in the chaos of movement, recording movement, starting with movements composed of the most complex combinations.

Freed from the rule of sixteen to seventeen frames per second, free of the limits of time and space. I put together any given points in the universe, no matter where I have recorded them.

My path leads to the creation of fresh perception of the world. I decipher in new ways a world unknown to you.[23]

The article is actually the first draft of a book which Vertov never finished. For the five years after this article was published Vertov was entirely involved in the realization of his philosophy about film *on* film; a new type of film entirely. In 1923 Vertov moved from discussions 'On the Significance of Newsreel'[24] to debates 'On the Significance of Unplayed Film'.[25] I have chosen very deliberately to translate the Russian term *neigrovaia fil'ma* as 'unplayed film'. The more usual translations will not suffice to explain Vertov's position. 'Non-acted' does not fully capture the investigative spirit of 'life caught unawares' (*zhizn' vrasplokh*). This term, coined by Vertov, contains a commitment to the 'skilful organization of the filmed factual world'.[26] Thus the other neutral term 'non-fiction' which would suggest that Vertov was seeking to present unmediated, unstaged reality will not do either. Vertov's own understanding of what the documentary project constituted is the main reason why the term 'unplayed' has been used throughout this study.

Throughout 1923 and 1924 Vertov was struggling to expand the possibilities of newsreel production. He and his team utilized animation (in both newsreel and the Cine-Truth series). They exploited various kinds of filming (particularly aerial photography), manipulation of shooting and projection speeds and, to a limited extent in Cine-Truth, montage technique. Nonetheless Vertov was increasingly frustrated by the limitations of short films so closely tied to the events of the day and yet still suffering from production delays which removed their immediate topicality anyway. Vertov worked on a new form of 'newsreel lightning' (*khronika-mol'niia*) which aimed to present material the day it was filmed. This attempt to pre-empt television news by some 30 years was doomed to failure but is evidence of the vision of its originator.

The final three films of the Cine-Truth series work as a trilogy. If seen as three parts of one film they signal Vertov's move into his classic period. Number 21 was made to mark the first anniversary of Lenin's death. Number 22 showed how the peasants remembered the great leader and number 23 (an especially clear illustration of the policy of 'link' (*smychka*) between the city and countryside) reported the coming of radio to a collective farm.

In 1924 Goskino felt confident enough in Vertov's talent, undoubted reputation and ability to produce films of impeccable political correctness to set up Kultkino (educational cinema) – a special documentary section – and to place Vertov in charge. Vertov was so confident of his own position that he could announce that Lenin's 'most important of all the arts' statement had been made with reference to documentary.[27] *The Man with the Movie Camera* can be seen as the culmination of a period where Vertov broke away from the restrictions of his early newsreel/Cine-Truth years to launch a series of extraordinary full-length films whilst running a vociferous campaign in defence of his own methodology. That period runs from the release of *The Cine-Eye* in October 1924 until the release of *The Man with the Movie Camera* in the spring of 1929.[28]

In 1924 Vertov made the quantum leap from newsreel and innovative short documentaries to works which stand as milestones in the history of cinema. *The Cine-Eye* even today appears as a remarkable film. The film begins, like *The Man with the Movie Camera*, with a statement of intent:

THE FIRST EXPLORATION OF
LIFE CAUGHT UNAWARES
THE FIRST NON-ARTIFICIAL CINEMA OBJECT
WITHOUT
SCENARIO
WITHOUT
ACTORS OR STUDIO

The titles fill the screen, grabbing the viewers' attention. An iris opens – the imagery is obvious but effective (and will be used often in Vertov's later films) – to reveal scenes of religious activity and village life. Much of *The Cine-Eye* is dedicated to proselytising the cooperative system. In a private market scene film of a pioneer's mother is run backwards to show *her* running backwards into the cooperative.

A section in the second reel deals with 'How the Chinese magician Xhan-Ti-Xhan earns his daily bread.' Children are entranced by a display of juggling and sleight of hand. In parallel, the viewer is treated to a show of editing and title construction. This sequence was utilized again in *The Man with the Movie Camera*. Other sequences from *The Cine-Eye* are experiments which reappear in the later film including the sequence entitled 'sleepers' which features 'life caught unawares' shots of various vagrants and a sequence of shots of Tverskaia Street taken from a moving camera. Much of this material is shown in reverse and speeded up. As in *The Man with the Movie Camera*, the cameraman joins an ambulance crew on an emergency call.

The whole film is an implicit criticism of the New Economic Policy. The linking of contrasts throughout the film seem to suggest that capitalism is a disease which has not yet been eradicated from Soviet society. Vertov, not for the first or last time, had made a film which did not fit easily with the political orthodoxy of the time. Ten years later that inability to show sufficient sensitivity to the political climate (with *Three Songs about Lenin* [Tri pesni o Lenine, 1934]) would be more damning to his career. The real problem for Vertov in 1924 was that the message was delivered in a visually complex manner. The viewer does have to work hard to create sense from the kaleidoscope of images. This uncompromising approach to cinema was likely to be as unpopular – even 'incomprehensible' as Vladimir Erofeyev described the film in his review.[29]

The Cine-Eye was widely acclaimed but, as for several of Vertov's later films, that acclaim came from *abroad*. The film was exported as an example of the advanced creativity that the Revolution had unleashed and nurtured. Thus it was exhibited as part of the Soviet exhibit at the International Trade Fair in Paris and received a diploma.

For the Cine-Eyes 1925 was a barren year in terms of film releases. It was however a year of frantic activity. In addition to more public debate about his position on the primacy of documentary, Vertov set about gaining commissions. Kultkino found not one but two customers. Gostorg (the Soviet Trade organization) required an advertising film. The Moscow City Soviet wanted a propaganda film to enthuse the home audience at the time of the election campaign.

With eight camera teams working on *One Sixth of the World* Vertov and Svilova worked on archive material while Kopalin and Beliakov filmed contemporary life in Moscow for *Forward Soviet!* After previews in March a campaign of support for *Forward Soviet!* developed in *Pravda* on 12 March, 16 May, 9 June and the morning after the official premiere took place on 23 July 1926.

As Vertov's confidence grew he threw himself into more vociferous and antagonistic campaigns. He was also engaged in writing a scenario for *Ten Years of October* [10 let oktiabria] and working on drafts for *The Man with the Movie Camera*, which developed an idea for *Forward Soviet!* and would begin with the city itself awakening.

For Vertov 1926 was distinguished by increasing attention. Much of it was critical. In addition he was to face increased competition from at least one genuinely great film-maker. Sergei Eisenstein had become a

7. The magician

serious competitor for domestic and international attention as well as
precious resources after *The Battleship Potemkin* [Bronenosets Potemkin,
released January 1926]. Typically of Vertov's character, he reacted to
increased pressure with increasingly vociferous certainty. Vertov's self-
publicity can be seen hitting its stride with 'The Factory of Facts' in
Pravda on 24 July 1926. The article's subtitle might have been 'By way
of a proposal' but it begins: 'The Cine-Eye method has now won out
completely.'[30]

It was this kind of arrogance that led to criticism even from close
friends and colleagues in the non-fiction 'camp'. In October 1926 Esfir
Shub attacked Vertov with an accusation of 'The Manufacture of
Facts':

We must object to the Cine-Eyes' monopoly.
    It is not only those who look at the USSR through the 'Cine-Eye
or who can narrate socialist construction exclusively in pathetic hits'
who want to work in non-played cinema.

Different facts must reach the studio.

The studio must take this into account, remove its Futuristic sign and become simply a factory for non-played cinema where people could work on editing newsreels, films of the history of the Revolution made from newsreel footage, where scientific production films and general cultural films could be made as a counterweight to played entertainment films.[31]

For Shub the manifestos – and militant anti-fiction campaigns – were over. It was time to work and to do so in a more prosaic, journalistic manner: 'We do not need a factory of facts if it is to manufacture facts.'[32]

Less sympathetic voices were raised against Vertov's method as a whole. Shklovsky attacked with 'Where is Dziga Vertov Striding?' in *Sovetskii ekran* [Soviet Screen] on 14 August 1926:

Dziga Vertov has done a great deal in Soviet cinema. It is due to him that new paths have opened up.
I had to see *Forward Soviet!*[33]

... A montage of everyday life? Life caught unawares. Not material of world importance. But I think that newsreel material is in Vertov's treatment deprived of its soul – its documentary quality.
A newsreel needs titles and date.
... Dziga Vertov cuts up newsreel. In this sense his work is not artistically progressive...[34]

One Sixth of the World was shown at the Fifteenth Party Congress in November before its public premiere on 31 December 1926. The film had received a good review in *Pravda* on 12 October. Vertov announced, in *Kino* no. 34, that to be against the film was to be against Soviet power. Nonetheless, some were only too willing to raise their voices in protest, including prominent critics such as Shklovsky – in 'The Cine-Eyes and Intertitles'[35] – who accused the film of being fiction. Shklovsky continued to make the same points at every opportunity in 1927.

Ippolit Sokolov was at least as forthright, criticizing the film as: 'the deformation of facts done by montage'.[36] In a point typical of the more pragmatic and business-like atmosphere of the film industry,

Sokolov also attacked Vertov's profligacy. The filming was 'accidental without a precise plan', the ratio of shooting to finished film was 20:1. Vertov would continue to defend this, admittedly high even for a documentary, ratio by the claim that he had several more films to make from the footage. Sokolov felt it was rather more due to 'chaos'. Sokolov saved the most damning point until last. Soviet films took on average a gross of 12–13 thousand roubles in their first week, *One Sixth of the World* took only 8,500. Sokolov was keen to point out that this was in a week that included two holidays.[37]

Vertov naturally responded with a personal attack:

> The unwillingness or rather *inability* to understand the structure of *One Sixth of the World* should not call forth surprise; it is by no means necessary for a specialist in the study of the lace on Mary Pickford's pantaloons to understand anything about the process of constructing the non-acted film.[38]

Sokolov's letter of response[39] was delayed by the editors but only served to confirm Nikolai Lebedev's claim[40] that Vertov had stolen parts of *Around Europe* [Po Evrope] and added Stepanov's *Kazakhstan* as well as, surely unbelievably, *With Iron and Blood* [Zhelezom i krov'iu] a fiction film by Vladimir Karin. Sokolov concluded triumphantly, '*One Sixth of the World* is not a superlative example of the non-acted film, but a poor example of fiction cinema.'[41]

The film was soon withdrawn from Soviet screens. It was shown widely abroad but to left-wing critics and film clubs, through the good offices of Mezhrabpom,[42] not the audience Gostorg needed for a film about trade. In fact the film was practically useless as propaganda for economic cooperation. Its absolutely overt and aggressive, political message was that trade consolidated and strengthened the population of the world's first socialist state: 'WHO OVERTHREW THE CAPITALISTS IN OCTOBER ... WHO DISCOVERED THE PATH TO A NEW LIFE?'

On 4 January 1927 Vertov was sacked by Sovkino, an organization always keen to show its businesslike credentials, as replacement for the discredited Goskino. We should remember that it was Goskino which had financed Vertov to work independently within Kultkino.

The directors of Sovkino even went so far as to write to the editors of *Kino-Front* to complain about Vertov's claims – given the authority

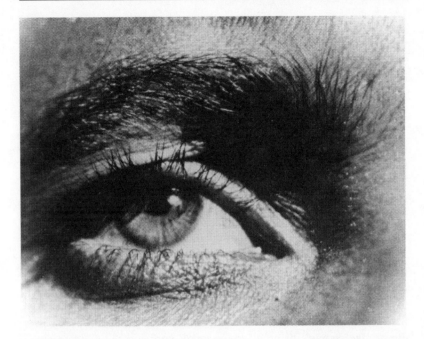

8. The eye

of print in *Kino* – that the film had been made efficiently. With a budget of 40,000 roubles (actually the budget was twice that) it was claimed Vertov had spent 130,000. It was in this (unpublished) letter that the threat to sack Vertov was made.[43] Vertov would be out of favour and out of work while the film industry received vast resources to celebrate the tenth anniversary of October.

By the time of Sokolov's damning publication, Vertov – perhaps forewarned – had retreated from the capital with criticisms and accusations ringing in his ears. The year 1927 was spent away from the sniping in Moscow. However, Vertov was not completing any work. He was not able to finish a full-length film in celebration of the tenth anniversary of the Revolution. By the end of 1927 Vertov was a man under pressure. Like Trotsky he looked on while the entity he had helped to create and believed that only he could nurture to its true potential – i.e. Soviet cinema – was being developed and exploited by others. It is *possible* to see the period after the tenth anniversary as a golden age for the non-fiction film makers in the Soviet Union. The increasingly powerful commissioning/funding system looked upon non-fiction film with some sympathy.

Esfir Shub had produced not one but two celebratory documentaries and taken Vertov's – long abandoned – genre of compilation film to new heights of subtlety and propaganda acumen with *The Fall of The Romanov Dynasty* [Padenie dinastii Romanovykh, released February 1927] and *The Great Way* [Velikii put', November 1927]. Shub had even re-edited some of the Cine-Eyes' newsreel material. She also showed a welcome ability to supply films which fulfilled their political brief, on budget and on time. So did Vertov's brother Mikhail Kaufman, who directed his own film *Moscow* [Moskva, December 1927]. This film was unsurprisingly very much a Cine-Eye production. The crew consisted of Kaufman, Kopalin, Beliakov and Zotov but Vertov was no longer leading them. Sovkino commissioned Kopalin and Beliakov to film the anniversary celebrations for *A Festival for the Millions* [Prazdnik millionov]. Iakov Bliokh's *Shanghai Document* [Shankhaiskii dokument] was to be one of the most popular Soviet films of 1928.[44] The film – based upon the footage taken by Stepanov during the 'people's rising' of the previous spring in the Chinese city – began its long and popular run in the capital on the May Day holiday. Bliokh was a representative of a new type of film-maker. He was a trained communist cadre (having joined the Party in 1918) who knew how to follow the Party line. Bliokh's film begins at a very slow pace – even compared with Shub at her most ponderous. The relative lack of text and the steady presentation would have made the film more readily understandable to the wider, less sophisticated audience both the industry and its political masters were seeking.

The Cultural Revolution, which would offer such an opportunity to film-makers, was also about to crush experimentation. The New Economic Policy became the *old* economic policy as a crash programme of industrialization required the collectivization of the whole agricultural sector. All propaganda media would be needed to engage the population as a whole in the new struggle ahead and to institute a cultural revolution. Thus, above and beyond the rivalry between film-makers, the whole atmosphere of the Soviet cinema, much as in Soviet politics and society, changed radically at the end of 1927.

The 15th Party Congress confirmed, as ever, the need to strengthen control over culture. The difference this time was more in the nature of the Congress[45] and the leading role played by the ever more powerful

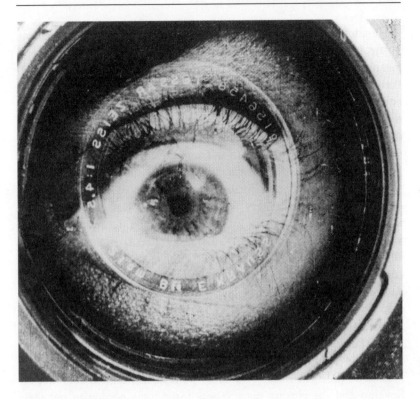

9. The Cine-Eye

Stalin. The Congress's call for action, and its general tone of impatience, found a compliant response in the film industry. In January the All-Union Conference of Cinematographic and Photographic Workers, encouraged by Lunarcharsky, could still plead for independence and reject the calls for purges in personnel.[46] However, the All-Union Party Conference on Cinema Affairs was to take a much firmer line when it was finally held in March 1928. The start was delayed due to the need for careful pre-planning including taking reports from Party cells and trade unions within the film industry which could be relied on to fit the political leadership's need for action to outweigh the opinions of the – soon to be purged, or at least hushed – professional elite. Youngblood states correctly that the Conference 'marks the end of an era. After it, the issues which had provoked genuine – if obstreperous – debate ossified into formulae.'[47]

Hanging over the Conference was the memory of Stalin's comment to the 13th Party Congress in May 1924: 'The cinema is the greatest means of mass agitation. The task is to take it into our own hands.'[48] Perhaps more pointed was the realization that the film industry itself had failed to fulfil its role. A. I. Krinitsky, head of the Agitprop Department of the Central Committee, made the keynote address. He stressed the need for the cinema to provide the 'high cultural level' necessary for the Cultural Revolution to accompany the first Five-Year Plan. Whilst praising the films which dealt with Revolutionary history (for which we can read Shub's documentaries) he poured scorn on the lack of films about contemporary Soviet life. Vertov should not have seen this as an encouragement for his Cine-Eye method. Krinitsky called for agitational (i.e. simple) shorts.[49] Krinitsky had formulated a slogan which would go on to haunt Soviet film-workers in the decades to come. Films should be: 'comprehensible to the millions' (*poniatny millionam*).[50] The debate which followed tended to confirm the view that Soviet cinema was in its usual state of civil war.[51] Krinitsky finished the first session of the Conference by telling the delegates to stop talking and get working: 'It is time to translate the Cultural Revolution from the skies of general judgements to the soil of systematic practical work.'[52] Later sessions turned critical attention on Sovkino and the cinema press. These institutions needed to put their own houses in order quickly. In this they failed. The industry and its journals were about to go through major restructuring.

Richard Taylor sums up the Conference thus:

> The general message of the Conference was unambiguous: the Party and the Soviet public must take the Soviet cinema in hand. The cinema must be made into a weapon of the internal class struggle being waged during the Cultural Revolution of the First Five Year Plan.[53]

The Party's attention had turned with force upon 'the most important of all the arts.' The *Sovetskii ekran* [Soviet Screen] editorial (18 December 1928) damned 'Formalist madness, the play on the "film shot" and its combination' (i.e. montage) and noted that:

> Given correct leadership, given the presence of a clear Party line in our cinema, given the tireless promotion of new young and healthy

cadres from both the film workers and the mass audience, cinema will successfully fulfil a powerful role in the Cultural Revolution.[54]

The 12 December *Sovetskii ekran* had reported the resolution of the Sovkino Workers' Conference. The resolution called for a much more formalized control of film activity from film school to the studios as well as *'artistic expression that is intelligible to the millions'*.[55] The Central Committee was poised to issue its decree 'On the Strengthening of Cinema Cadres'.[56] Proletarianization was under way with all of its opportunities – and dangers.

Sovetskii ekran editorials of early 1929 made it clear that the cinema was crucial to the project of 'cultural revolution'.[57] The need for accessibility was also stressed, for example, in an article celebrating the 200th edition of the Sovkino newsreel *Sovkinozhurnal*:

[Non-fiction film] can and must address the millions. And its language? Through simplicity and accessibility, through clarity and ingenuity, through evident visual directness ...[58]

The term 'simply and clearly' (*prosto i iasno*) became the slogan of the cinema press. This was the very month that Vertov, with his usual supremely bad timing, was exhibiting one of the most challenging and visually sophisticated films in the history of world cinema, *The Man with the Movie Camera*.

Vertov had rushed way ahead even of his few admirers. When praise for his work did appear, it was for four-year-old films. Another (non-related) Kaufman praised the Cine-Eyes in January 1929 comparing their work – as a cultural artefact – to the cathedral at Rheims:

Nothing can replace a single copy of the *Lenin CinePravda,* for the photographic newsreel of our day is a document of first-rate importance through which future generations will be able to study the living history of our days.[59]

Vertov, who had been absent from Moscow for over a year, did not attend the conferences and congresses that changed Soviet cinema. He could have done nothing about the new direction being taken but he found himself both divorced as well as protected from the developments in Moscow. This was due to his new post in the Ukraine. VUFKU (the All-Ukrainian Photo-Cinema Administration) was second only to Sovkino in terms of resources and well-established as a film producer since 1923. Vertov was to gain the advantage of animosity between the 'big two' companies and could play on the fact that the Ukrainian administrators saw the 'poaching' of Vertov as a victory over their Moscow rivals (who they had been fighting to keep autonomy from since the setting up of Sovkino).

Vertov had gathered the rest of the 'Council of Three' around him and had the (Kultkino) rights to a considerable library of footage shot for previous films. His first commission was to make a film for the tenth anniversary of the October Revolution. However the time simply was not available. Neither were his best cameramen: Kaufman, Zotov and Kopalin were still working in Moscow. Vertov turned this lamentable situation into an artistic and propaganda advantage by seeking to make a film which, rather than looking back, looked forward to the next decade. Thus he was able to work feverishly on completing *The Eleventh Year* [Odinnadtsatyi] once Kaufman arrived in time to shoot the production processes in the mines and factories along the Dnieper which formed the film's diegesis.

The film was released on 15 May 1928. Less than six months later Vertov was ready to unleash *The Man with the Movie Camera*.[60] He had been toying with the idea from, at least, the time of *The Cine-Eye* and was already working seriously on his masterpiece before the release of *The Eleventh Year*. 'The Man with the Movie Camera (A Visual Symphony)' is a proposal for the film dated 19 March 1928:

The Man with the Movie Camera constitutes an experiment in the cinematic transmission of visual phenomena without the aid of intertitles (a film with no intertitles), script, (a film with no script), theatre (a film with neither actors nor sets).

Cine-Eye's new experimental work aims to create a truly international film language, *absolute writing in film* and the complete separation of cinema from theatre and literature.[61]

Vertov also reflected on the film in notes for an article: 'Man with the Movie Camera'. The notes were also written in 1928 and by their content – including references to debates after showings – were clearly written after the filming:

Work on *The Man with the Movie Camera* required greater effort than previous work of the Cine-Eye. This can be explained by the greater number of locations under observation as well as by complex organizational and technical operations while filming. The montage experiments demanded exceptional effort. These experiments went on constantly.[62]

It should be noted that Vertov is stressing the *montage* experiments. He goes on to argue that the lack of titles should not be a surprise. This is but a logical development from the Cine-Eye method and his more recent films (particularly *The Eleventh Year*):

> *The Man with the Movie Camera* represents not only a practical result. It is as well a theoretical manifestation on the screen. That is apparently why public debates on it in Kharkov and Kiev assumed the aspect of a fierce battle between representatives of various trends in so-called art. Moreover the dispute took place on several levels at once. Some said that the *The Man with the Movie Camera* was an experiment in visual music, a visual concert. Others saw the film in terms of a high mathematics of montage. Still others declared that it was not 'life as it is' but life the way they did not see it etc.[63]

Vertov passes down to us what he thought the film was. This passage is a – if not *the* – key to understanding the film:

> In fact the film is only the sum of the facts recorded on film, or if you prefer, not merely the sum but the product, a 'higher mathematics' of facts. Each term or each factor is a separate little document. The documents have been joined with one another so that, on the one hand, the film would consist only of those linkages between signifying pieces that coincide with the visual linkages and so that, on the other hand, these linkages would not require inter-titles, the final sum of all these linkages represents an organic whole.[64]

We have a snap-shot of Vertov's state of mind between the first showings of *The Man with the Movie Camera* and the prestigious Moscow Hermitage premiere. 'From Cine-Eye to Radio-Eye' is an unpublished article written in February 1929.

At first, from 1918 to 1922, the Cine-Eye was singular, there was only one Cine-Eye. From 1923 to 1925 there were already three or four. From 1925 on the Cine-Eye's ideas became more clearly known. As the original group grew the number of member-popularizers of the movement grew. It is now possible to speak not only of group but of a school, not only of a sector of a front but of a whole front of unplayed cinematography.[65]

Vertov then gives an insight into his working method, including the interesting idea that he equates *editing* alone with organization. It should be noted that Vertov sees 'editing' occurring at *every* stage of film-making.:

The Cine-Eye = cine-seeing (I see through the camera) + cine-writing (I write on film with the camera) + cine-organization (I edit)...

The Cine-Eye plunges into the seething chaos of life to find life itself.

The response to an assigned theme. To find the resultant force amongst the million phenomena related to a given theme. To edit, to draw out through the camera what is most typical and most useful from life; to organize the shots extracted from life into a meaningful rhythmic visual order, a meaningful visual phrase, the essence of 'I see.'

Every Cine-Eye production is subject to montage from the moment the theme is chosen until the film's release in its completed form...

Within this continuous process of editing we can distinguish three stages: The first stage: editing is the inventory of all documentary data directly or indirectly related to the assigned theme ... the plan of the theme crystallizes, becomes clear, emerges in the editing process.

The second stage: editing is the human eye's summing up of observations on the assigned theme ... (this leads) to a shooting plan, as a result of selecting and sorting the human eye's observations. In making this selection, the author takes into account the indications of the thematic plan as well as the special properties of the 'machine-eye' and the 'Cine-Eye'.

The third stage: central editing – the summary of observations recorded on film by the Cine-Eye. A numerical calculation of the montage groupings.

The combining (addition, subtraction, multiplication, division and factoring out) of related pieces. There is a continual shifting of the pieces until they are all placed in a rhythmical order so that all links of meaning coincide with the visual links. As the final result of all this blending, shifts and cancellations we achieve a visual equation or visual formula.[66]

It is interesting that here, as he gets to the crux of his cinematic method, Vertov's written language begins to let him down. He is not sure if either the word equation or formula is quite right. I would contend that 'coincide' does not adequately explain the relationship between meaning and visual image. It is simply too difficult to separate all the resonant and harmonious mix of factors. Vertov's cinematic language has become so rich that it can only be understood in cinematic terms.

In this passage of 'Cine-Eye to Radio-Eye' Vertov is expostulating on his 'theory of intervals' – the use of musical metaphors is both obvious and to be expected. In his first manifesto 'We', Vertov wrote:

The organization of movement is the organization of its elements, or its intervals, into phrases.

In each phrase there is a rise, a high point and a falling off (to varying degrees) of movement.

A composition is made of phrases, just as a phrase is made of intervals of movement.

It was in 'We' that Vertov made explicit the point that: 'Intervals [are] the transitions from one movement to another'.[67] The central importance of this concept was made in 'The Cine-Eyes – A Revolution': 'it is entirely a question of the particular juxtaposition of visual details – of intervals.'[68] Vertov is giving his audience specific instructions to watch (above all) for the matches on (or across) movement throughout the film. Then we will experience how:

This formula, this equation, obtained as a result of the general montage of the recorded film-documents *is* a 100 per cent film-object, the concentrated essence of 'I see' – I cine-see.'[69]

Two days after writing 'From Cine-Eye to Radio-Eye' Vertov gave a talk 'From the History of the Cine-Eyes' in which he made two very important points when he discussed *The Battle for Tsaritsyn* : 'It was done with very fast montage and no titles. It was so to speak, the ancestor of *The Cine-Eye* and *The Man with the Movie Camera*.'[70] Vertov clearly links those two films in his *own* mind confirming the view of *The Man with the Movie Camera* as not only the culmination of the Cine-Eyes' career 1918–28 but also as the product of frenzied – if frustrated – activity from 1925 to 1928 i.e. from *The Cine-Eye* to *The Man with the Movie Camera's* execution. This period is framed by two films with many similarities which Vertov himself was happy to recognize. The critical point is that, although *The Man with the Movie Camera* could be viewed as *Cine-Eye II* because the connections are clear, the development is exponential.

Leyda, as usual, spotted this – whilst admittedly taking a rather more critical tone than mine:

> The structure resembles that of Kino-Eye, with a succession of themes … but the execution of the two films, separated by less than five years, are worlds apart. The camera observation in Kino-Eye was alert, surprising, but never eccentric. Things were 'caught' but less for the catching's sake than for close observation of the things themselves. In *The Man with the Movie Camera* all the stunts that can be performed by a cameraman armed with a debrie or hand-camera (sic) and by a film-cutter armed with the boldness of Vertov and Svilova can be found in this full to bursting film.[71]

Some modern critics (including this one) would dissent from the implied accusation of pure formalism. Nonetheless this film has never been more accurately described than as 'full to bursting…' When Leyda got to know Vertov in Moscow in 1934, he was surprised at how bitter and sad the great master had become. He met Vertov at a time when the frustrations of his career had overwhelmed him. At the time of *The Man with the Movie Camera* Vertov's sense of alienation from the rest of film industry, his reaction to two years of disappointment and a context of political crisis produced a masterpiece.

In 'From the History of the Cine-Eyes' Vertov also makes crucial points on the subject of structure : 'Measurement went not according to the metrical system but by a decimal system of frames.'[72] I have

taken this very precise approach to sequence length as one of the justifi-
cations for my structural reading of the film in the next chapter.[73]

The rest of the article is a fervent rant about the frustrations of
working in a bureaucratic and insensitive system. As such it is apiece
with the opinions of any – every? – movie director who has ever lived.
More pertinently they do not just catalogue Vertov's past problems,
they are evidence of a growing frustration which had reached the
heights of intensity by the time of *The Man with the Movie Camera*.

Vertov's masterpiece left Soviet screens very quickly never to return.
However the film received a good deal of attention in Europe and the
United States. Vertov was sent on tour with *The Man With the Movie
Camera* and became a well-known representative of a Soviet avant-
garde that was no longer required at home. Vertov's high international
profile made him the ideal candidate to make the first sound documen-
tary *Enthusiasm* or *Symphony of the Donbas* [Entuziazm a.k.a. Simfoniia
Donbassa, 1931]. Again the film was not widely distributed in the
Soviet Union but achieved fame abroad.

Vertov's career as a cultural diplomat for the Soviet Union fixed his
Western image as a vociferous personality in the artistic avant-garde. It
is a view which has remained unchallenged since the 1930s. Vertov
remained a famous figure, to many (including, according to Vertov,
Charlie Chaplin)[74] *the* international face of Soviet cinema.

At home Vertov remained tolerated until he finally blotted his
copybook beyond redemption by offending Stalin with the original cut
of *Three Songs about Lenin* which had failed to mention the 'Great
Leader' Stalin at all. Vertov could offend other film-makers and fritter
away valuable resources on experimental sound montage but offending
the leader was a step too far. No matter what depths of hagiography
Vertov could plumb later in the 1930s, for example *Lullaby* [Kolybel-
naia, 1937], he was never to be completely trusted again.

This crucial mistake is the clearest example of Vertov's political
naivety. His lack of ability to follow his masters' 'general line' should not
lead us to see Vertov as non- or apolitical. It is valid to suggest that the
Soviet masters – including Vertov – should be seen as *political* film-
makers (however flawed in the execution of their masters' aims). They all
certainly claimed to be making political films. Vertov was explicit as any:

The basis of our programme is not film production for entertainment or profit (which we leave to artistic drama), but a film bond

between the peoples of the USSR and the entire world based on a platform of the communist decoding of what actually is.[75]

The central thrust of this 'communist decoding' was changing drastically in the period 1928–9. In *The Man with the Movie Camera* Vertov produced a film that was a product of personal, artistic and cinematic crisis made against a back-drop of domestic and international political turmoil and the beginnings of a social and economic maelstrom. The greatness of *The Man with the Movie Camera* in cinematic terms will be explained and explored in the following chapter. The close textual analysis also makes regular reference to the political points being made by Vertov's choice of material and method of presentation.

Notes

1 D. Vertov, 'Kinoki, perevorot' in S. Drobashenko ed., *Dziga Vertov: Stat'i, dnevniki, zamysli* (Moscow, 1966) p. 55. Throughout this book I will use my own translations of Vertov's writings taken from Drobashenko (referred to as *SD*). Where possible I have used Richard Taylor's excellent translations of several of Vertov's most important statements as contained in *The Film Factory* – these will be indicated by *FF* and page number. For readers who wish to refer to full (American) English translations I will also give references to O'Brien trans., *Kino-Eye – The Writings of Dziga Vertov* as *KE* and page numbers.
   Thus for this quote: *KE* p. 18, *FF* p. 93.
2 Cited in R. Taylor, *The Politics of Soviet Cinema*, Cambridge, 1979, p. 643.
3 A similar tendency towards impatience with diversity occurred in the arts with the formation and subsequent banning of Proletkul't.
4 G. Hosking, *A History of the Soviet Union*, London, 1992, p. 136.
5 e.g. the final set of titles in Vertov's *The Eleventh Year* begins: 'to the victory of socialism in our country...'
6 Hosking, p. 138.
7 Stalin's strategy had also weakened control over the Chinese communists. Mao split with Moscow on ideological as well as practical grounds. He began to develop his belief that socialism would depend on the peasants.
8 R. Sakwa, *Soviet Politics*, London, 1989, p. 41.
9 Hosking, p. 150.
10 see V. Lenin *On Imperialism*, London, 1974.
11 Vertov had used a speech by Stalin: 'We want to make ... not only processed cotton ... but the machines necessary for processing cotton ... we want to make ... not only tractors ... but machines for making tractors...' to illustrate the need for machine tools in the final reel of *One Sixth of the Earth*.

12   Vertov on occasion gave his date of birth as 1897.

13   This explains why his patronymic is different from that of his brother Mikhail Abramovich Kaufman.

14   In 'The Birth of the Cine-Eye' published in 1924 Vertov refers to 'fantastic novels (*The Iron Hand, An Uprising in Mexico*)' as well as essays, poems and 'epigrams and satirical verse'. *SD* p. 73, *KE* p. 40.

15   In fact Vertov had been considering involvement with moving pictures for at least a year before that. In a poem entitled 'Start' he expressed his excitement with 'KINO' [cinema]. See V. Listov 'Pervyi fil'm Dzigi Vertova' *Prometii*, 1966, p. 128.

16   *SD* p. 73, *KE* p. 40.

17   Letter to Steven Hill published in *Film Culture* 44, 1967. p. 00.

18   'Cine-Eye' *SD* p. 91, *KE* p. 61.

19   Vertov's other brother emigrated to France with his parents in 1919. He went on to work as a cinematographer with Jean Vigo (*Zéro de conduite*, 1933 and *L'Atalante*, 1934) and others, including Abel Gance (*Lucrèce Borgia*, 1934), before working with great distinction in Hollywood (e.g. Elia Kazan's *On the Waterfront*, 1954, *Baby Doll* 1956 and *Splendor in the Grass*, 1959 and many of Sidney Lumet's films of the 1950s and 1960s including *Twelve Angry Men*, 1957 and *Long Day's Journey into Night*, 1962).

20   *SD* pp. 45–48, *FF* pp. 69–71, *KE* pp. 5–9.

21   as *Dziga Vertov: Stat'i, dnevniki, zamysli.*

22   *SD* pp. 52–3 , *KE* pp. 15–7 *FF* p. 91.

23   *SD* pp. 54–5, *KE* pp. 17–8, *FF* p. 93.

24   In a talk to *Proletarian Cinema* April 1923 see *SD* p. 67, *KE* p. 32.

25   Vertov's use of this term to describe his methodology begins with 'The film known as *The Cine-Eye*' (a request to Goskino to make the film) and 'On the significance of unplayed cinema' (a contribution to a debate at the Association of Workers in Revolutionary Cinematography) – both 1923. See *SD* pp. 68–71, *KE* pp. 34–38.

26   'Artistic Drama and the Cine-Eye', contribution to a debate of July 1924 *SD* p. 80, *KE* p. 48, *FF* pp. 115–116.

27   see for example '*Kinopravda and Radiopravda*', *Pravda*, July 16, 1925 SD p. 84–86, KE pp. 52–56.

28   It is possible to argue that Vertov's militant – and most creative – period stretches as far as the making of *Enthusiasm* and his being caught up in the ensuing campaigns against 'documentalism' (see *Forward Soviet!* pp. 93–104). Post 1932 Vertov in his film-making and attempts at self-justification appears an increasingly sad and weary man.

29   *Kino-gazeta*, 21 October 1924.

30   *SD* p. 87, *KE* p. 58, *FF* p. 150.

31   *FF* p. 152.

32   ibid.

33   'Shagai' could be translated as 'stride' as well as 'forward,' even as '(stride) forward.' Thus the title of Shklovskii's article is a pun.

34 *FF* p. 151–2.

35 *FF* p. 153.

36 *Kino-Front* 2, 1927 translation from D. Youngblood, *Soviet Cinema in the Silent Era* (Austin, 1991). pp. 140–1.

37 I should point out the film also had the benefit of a high profile opening at Moscow's most prestigious cinema on Malaia Dmitrovka.

38 Translation from Youngblood, p. 141. Youngblood's cataloguing of the highly personalized disagreements between the personalities of Soviet cinema in the 1920s and 1930s is unrivalled, as is the depth of her knowledge of the institutional changes taking place in the mid-to-late 1920s.

39 *Kino-Front* 7/8 1927 pp. 31–2.

40 *Kino-Front* 3 1927 p. 2.

41 ibid. pp. 31–2.

42 'International Workers' Aid', from which the acronym Mezhrabpom is derived, based in Germany, served as conduit for material support for the Soviet state and as a distributor for Soviet cultural products.

43 Youngblood p. 157.

44 See N. J. Cull and A. Waldron, 'Shanghai Document – *"Shankhaiskii dokument"* (1928): Soviet Film Propaganda and the Shanghai Rising of 1927', *Historical Journal of Film, Radio and Television*, 16, no. 3, 1996, pp. 323–46.

45 See pp. 10–11.

46 R. Taylor *The Politics of the Soviet Cinema 1917–1929*, Cambridge, 1979, pp. 105–6.

47 Youngblood, p. 157.

48 Quoted in Taylor, p. 108.

49 Krinitsky was returning to Plekhanov's separation of propaganda and agitation (*agitatsiia*) as 'only a few ideas ... to a whole mass of people'. See *Forward Soviet!* pp. 13–15.

50 Taylor, p. 108.

51 see Taylor, pp. 109–10 and *FF* pp. 205–15.

52 Taylor, p. 111.

53 Taylor, p. 118.

54 'O pravoi opasnosti v kino,' *Sovetskii ekran*, 18 December 1928, (*FF* p. 246).

55 A full translation of this resolution is printed in *FF* pp. 241–5.

56 *FF* pp. 253–4.

57 e.g. the editorial to no. 16 16/4/29 'Kino na sluzhbu kul'turnoi revolutsii' which calls for a 'cinefication of the countryside'.

58 'Glubzhe v zhizn'', *Sovetskii ekran*, 23 April 1929.

59 N. Kaufman 'Kinoki', *Sovetskii ekran*, 18 January 1929.

60 It is certainly worth reminding ourselves what a year 1929 was for Soviet cinema. Apart from *The Man with the Movie Camera*, Dovzhenko released *The Arsenal* [Arsenal] in February. The FEKS unleashed the equally astonishing *New Babylon* [Novyi Vavilon] in March. In October the 'unplayed' produced *Turksib* whilst an audience finally saw Eisenstein's *The Old and the New* [Staroe i novoe].

61 *SD* pp. 277–9, *KE* pp. 283–9.
    I will utilize this proposal throughout my textual analysis of the film in the next chapter.
62 *SD* p. 106–108, *KE* pp. 82–85.
63 ibid p. 108, p. 85.
64 ibid.
65 *SD* p. 110, *KE* p. 87.
66 *SD* pp. 110–111, *KE* pp. 87–88.
67 *SD* p. 46, *KE* p. 8, *FF* p. 71.
68 *SD* p. 57, *KE* p. 21 *FF* p. 94.
69 *SD* p. 115, *KE* p. 90.
70 *SD* p. 117, *KE* pp. 93.
71 Leyda, p. 251.
72 *SD* pp. 117–123, *KE* pp. 93–100.
73 That does not mean to say I will take a purely decimal approach (although certain lengths, and repetitions of lengths, of sequences will be analysed). Rather I have taken Vertov at his word that length, down to precise calculations of the number of frames in a particular shot or sequence, is important.
74 D. Vertov, 'Charli Chaplin, Gamburgskie rabochie i prikazy Doktora Virta', *Proletarskoe kino*, no. 3, 1932.
75 *SD* p. 82, *KE* p. 50.

3. A Textual Analysis

Berlin and *Rien que les heures* – forget all that.

Oswell Blakeston, 1929[1]

My path leads to the creation of a fresh perception of the world. I can thus decipher a world that you do not know.

Dziga Vertov 1923[2]

The aim of the following close reading is to confront the images directly. To think clearly and closely about what Vertov and his team present and how they present it. This is done by the choice of individual shots and by the choice of particular subjects and *mise-en-scène* in general. In addition it is essential to pay close attention to how shots are constructed and framed to produce their – and by extension our – point of view. For this film, perhaps more than any other, it is crucial to study how shots are cut to length and connected and how sequences are put together. I will pay particular attention to the structure of sequences, larger overarching sections and the whole film as a diegesis. At all times my underlying question will remain; why is Vertov doing this?

The three methods of approach – sequential, sectional and thematic – differ in their focus but work together to elucidate the meanings of the film:

Sequential analysis

This method still sees the film as a 66 minute whole but attempts to discern sequences of action that can be read as narratives in themselves or fragments of a larger narrative. This is the way that a viewer might see and respond to the film on first viewing. As this process of apprehension is described I will attempt to aid comprehension by indicating the deeper structures and visual/material relationships which are occurring and being built as the film runs.

Vlada Petrić[3] identifies 55 'units' in 1,682 shots. In terms of 'units' – I prefer episodes – my analysis is based on 16 such episodes, preceded by a 'prologue' or 'overture.'

Sectional analysis

The conventional way of sectioning films is in reels. The following reading will not ignore that most physical of divisions. However, it is important to note that viewers do not watch for reel ends/beginnings. By 1929 many theatres would have had the facilities to avoid a break in projection to 'change reels'. It is just as important to remember that the film-maker is not working in terms of 'reels' at all, except in general terms of the approximate length of the film. My analysis is sectioned in terms of temporal duration.

The focus for these temporal periods is a series of key points through the film. I have sectioned the film at mid-way, quarters, thirds and tenths (and indeed twentieths) of duration to reveal the power – and point – of its use of time. Particular attention is drawn to the quarter and third points of the film. In general terms it is possible to see the shots at these points as particularly significant and thematically connected. Shots at tenths (six minutes 40 seconds) appear to be about 'setting in motion.' Shots at twelfths (five minutes 30 seconds) make more overtly political points. When these intervals coincide e.g. at quarter or half points the connections are doubly made and/or the film moves on. Admittedly many of these effects only become apparent on repeated viewing. I hope that my reading will help the viewer to begin the process on initial or early viewing.

On a micro (as well as a macro level) we must also take note of Vertov's 'theory of intervals'. This approach was most explicitly set out in 'The Cine-Eyes – A Revolution' written at the time of the film's premiere. It was in 'We' that Vertov first made explicit the point that: 'Intervals [are] the transitions from one movement to another.' Therefore we should be watching above all for the matches on (or across) movement throughout the film.

The necessity of very close attention – simultaneously to what is on the screen, what was on the screen and attempting to think about what is still to come – makes *The Man with the Movie Camera* a very demanding film. It demands that the spectator take an active role as decipherer. However an understanding of what to look out for – and Vertov gave plenty of instructions – should aid in the active enjoyment of the film.

Yuri Tsivian uses an entirely apposite phrase when he talks about the need for 'a completely topological grasp'[4] of the film. In the following pages I am trying to do that for the viewer. Like all great films, you do have to watch *The Man with the Movie Camera* again and again to gain more and more insights. Like all great art the film needs close textual and contextual reading to reveal its truths. Nonetheless, the film's temporal segmentation works to produce direct effects. The deliberate placing of particular images at particular points in time, juxtaposed by their kinetic content, *do* make clear filmic and political points and, if the viewer is forewarned and forearmed with a little information, *The Man with the Movie Camera* can be pleasurable as well as educational.

My temporal sectioning of the film is based on a timing of 66 minutes 30 seconds, i.e. including the manifesto as an integral part of the movie. Sectioning of the film based on and beginning with the moving pictures only is entirely unsatisfactory e.g. adjusting the timing of the film to 65 minutes 16 seconds gives a 1/4 point of 16 minutes 19 seconds after the titles, i.e. the middle of a mid-shot of some dresses. We can thus conclude that, not surprisingly, the manifesto is an integral part of the film.

Thematic analysis

This focuses on how particular images are repeated. A process of repetition, juxtaposition and rejuxtaposition are crucial to Vertov's methodology. It is through identifying the elements highlighted in this process of construction that it is possible to identify Vertov's themes. I will continue to argue that these themes are essentially political. Mikhail Kaufman – forgetting he was the star of *The Man with the Movie Camera*, rather than its creative director – never understood his brother's methodology:

> Do you remember that interminable number of trams, those repetitions? Well, one should never have so many repetitions. Things have to move forwards in some direction.[5]

Repetition of images is a key to cinema language, in films and between films (as well as through a genre and in *auteur* theory). Vertov understood this and utilized the method intelligently and consistently to make political points by building the depth of his signification in the repetition of imagery to build on already existing iconography. It is not too fanciful to suggest that his repetitions are an attempt to write and disseminate his own iconography.

My aim in the following pages is the close observation of a stream of images with regular reference to what Vertov said he was doing: in 'The Man with the Movie Camera (A Visual Symphony)'.[6] I will also constantly keep in mind the fact that Vertov believed himself to be a *political* film-maker. As he wrote in 'The Birth of the Cine-Eye,'[7] his aim was to: 'further the battle for the communist decoding of the world'. At all times the viewer should remember that the film really needs to be thought of as running at 24fps.

The Man with the Movie Camera begins with a bold statement – the only set of titles used in the film. The layout and content of the titles is worth close scrutiny. They are after all the only ones in the film. They are also a manifesto – our only clue as to what the purpose of this film is. Throughout my analysis I intend to take Vertov at his word. Therefore I believe the titles are useful to us as analysts because they constitute a clear exposition of what Vertov and his team believed they were doing. With this so extraordinary film – almost wilfully divorced from the traditions and institutions of film-making – this statement is of unique importance. As such it is worth a second reading to tease out Vertov's meanings and the very clear message he is giving his audience before any moving images appear.

Yuri Tsivian begins his analysis of the film by noting that the title is ironic. It apes the stock titles of movies like 'Man in the Iron Mask' and signals that this film is playful. The visual diegesis begins with plays on the notion of fiction and non-fiction. However, the manifesto that precedes the moving pictures is a brutal statement of intent.

I

MAN
THE MOVIE CAMERA
A record on celluloid
in 6 reels
Produced by VUFKU

1929
(An excerpt from the diary
of a cameraman)

II

ATTENTION
VIEWER:
This film
presents
an experiment[8]
in the cine-transmission[9]
of visible events

III

WITHOUT THE AID
OF CAPTIONS

(A film without intertitles/captions)

IV

WITHOUT THE AID
OF A SCENARIO
(A film without scenario)

V

WITHOUT THE AID
OF THEATRE
(A film without sets,
actors etc.)

VI

This experimental
work is directed
at the creation of a totally
international
absolute language
of cinema founded on its
total separation
from the language of theatre
and literature

VII [this caption is on screen for 4 seconds]
Author-supervisor
of the experiment
DZIGA VERTOV

VIII [3 seconds]
Chief cameraman
M. KAUFMAN [no first name]
XIV [3 seconds]
Assisting editor
E. SVILOVA

The hierarchy expressed and terms used for the protagonists' roles are important. This manifesto makes it clear that *The Man with the Movie Camera* is Vertov's film. 'Supervisor' (*rukovoditel'*) also means leader and instructor. Kaufman is 'chief cameraman' (*glavnii operator*) but that is *all*. A cameraman does not have responsibility for decisions of *mise-en-scène* and cinematography. Svilova is only credited as assistant even in the editing (*assistent po montazhu*).

There are no more credits. In fact there is no more text in the form of titles. However, it is important to watch out for text contained in the film's images. Signs in particular give the film a sense of anchorage. The title sequence lasts 1 minute 12 seconds and 12 frames. The moving images begin at 01.14.10. Thus the screen is blank for almost 2 seconds. A simple but effective way to build tension.

Throughout this reading timings will be given in minutes, seconds and frames on the left-hand side of the page. Timings are taken using the BFI video version.

The Prologue/Overture
1.14.10 – 1.24.23   The cameraman mounts a giant camera in a 'split screen' effect.
1.24.24 – 1.26.14   The top of a building with flagpole is silhouetted against the sky.
At 1.30.01 Kaufman (the cameraman) starts to carry the camera away.
1.33.06   A streetlight is silhouetted against a dawn sky.
Clouds pass to give passage of time. They appear slightly speeded up due to the film running but not being exposed at 24 fps. The essential point is of course what speed Vertov wanted the film run at (24 fps)

which then gives us the relative speed of whatever Kaufman photographed. This very early shot also gives us our first clue that the film *should* be run at 24 fps.

1.35.22	A curtain with the shadow of Kaufman (carrying a tripod) fully in view at 1.37.0 – Kaufman has passed behind curtain by 1.38.20.
1.40.12	A darkened theatre,
1.55.01	A cinema light,
1.55.10	A theatre aisle showing roped off entrance [including a close-up of the rope from 1.58.22 to 1.59.21].

This image clearly signals that the film will focus on a close examination of even the most (apparently) unimportant details.

2.02.01	The projector – at 2.09.01 the projectionist arrives.
2.10.12	He examines reels of film. In a supremely self-referential moment the label on the film can reveals it to be *The Man with the Movie Camera*.

The label on the film container gives textual anchorage yet states the impossible. The diegesis of *The Man with the Movie Camera* cannot contain projection of the finished film. By now the viewer should realize that they are in for a testing hour and six minutes.

2.13.14	A curtain – which is pulled back at 2.14.06 to reveal a chandelier.
2.14.12	The projector again – the film is being spooled.
2.16.19	Close up of the spool and projectionist,
2.19.10	Fade up to curtain – fingers appear bottom centre to pull a string at 2.20.12. The pulling action is matched by:
2.23.05	Chairs – pulled down and ready at 2.25.01.
2.26.06	A projector sprocket,
2.27.24	Blackout,
2.28.00	A hand reaches to undo the rope.
2.29.04	An unmatched cut to the theatre interior: the audience file in.

The viewer has been welcomed into the film's diegesis. We are invited to join the audience on screen. The film looks popular – but N.B. this audience is not actually one for *The Man with the Movie Camera*

2.31.09	The seats again – upright and down,

2.35.01	The crowd fills the seats.
2.39.01	The seats concertina in split screen.
2.42.06	The crowd is shown from crowd level.
2.46.08	A single seat comes down.
2.47.15	The crowd settling in their places.
2.52.01	A seat comes down (at an opposing angle).
2.54.22	The seat is down and a person approaches (screen right) with a child.
2.58.01	The crowd is seated.

Now the point of view is from the screen (i.e. in front and above)

3.01.18	A chandelier – seen from below – fades to black.
3.05.20	The conductor is poised.

The following shots are of orchestral players poised to play. The shots are not stills but give the impression that they are (unless you *look closely*). At 3.19.20 [1/20 point of the film] there is a cut from a horn player to a kettle drummer. The images are still but the cut instils action.

3.30.20	Two 'prongs' are coming together.

The viewer is bound to ask what they are.

3.32.12	The projectionist adjusting ...

What? More tension/expectation is created.

3.33.15	The prongs cut to the projectionist at 3.34.09

3.34.17/18	Black
3.34.19	The prongs come together. At 3.34.22 there is a spark and the projectionist's face is illuminated by the projector lamp.

Vertov is not just offering us a lesson in film-making. He wants to show us everything, including how film is projected. His technique has given even this, usually ignored, process drama. He reminds the viewer that film projection *is* magic. To me this section is a reminder of that magic. It also reveals that Vertov is as much the child of Méliès as the Lumières, however much he might deny it.

3.38.01	The projectionist moves. He is active and precise.
3.41.01	The conductor moves.

He has been *given movement* by film. At 3.42.06 the trombonist moves in response to conductor's arms coming *down*. The instrument's slide moves *across* (right to left). The film cross-cuts between trombone and violin. The tympani return at 3.47.01 and the whole band is visible at 3.54.01. Exactly 24 frames later the film is in motion through the projector

3.56.12   Fade up to the conductor [surely a visual metaphor for Vertov].

3.57.18   Black screen. The numeral '1' rises to vertical at 3.59.01

The film is now four minutes old and the moving pictures have been on screen for 2 minutes and 46 seconds. Yet such a vast amount of information has already been communicated it is worth stopping and considering what we have been told.

The Man with the Movie Camera has already informed the viewers that they are about to experience a completely new and *completely cinematic* form of communication. The power of filming 'life caught unawares' in a cinema has been used to show how film is projected to an audience whilst games are played with the notion of moving pictures. Truly, the medium is the message.

I have dwelt in such great detail on this 'Prologue' because this opening salvo in Vertov's visual assault is important to how the film will (and is expected) to affect the audience. Shocked and intrigued by the prologue, the viewer is prepared for the voyage ahead.

Episode 1: 'Wake up!'

This begins as an exercise in voyeurism.

4.00.02   Opens onto a window (mid-shot, slightly to screen left).

The camera is now mobile – zooming in.

The camera zooms and tracks through a curtained window. This image is an early reiteration of a repeated motif of the film: that the actions of the camera can reveal the previously hidden truth. Even more profound truths can be revealed by the illuminating power of editing.

4.09.22   Street-lights,

4.12.19   A woman in bed – the frame is slightly irised onto her arm.

4.17.12   A genre painting – full screen. The old man's stare directs the viewer to:

4.20.05   Detail – the woman's ring.

It is possible that Vertov is making comparisons between cinema and another visual art. He may even be making a statement (which we may assume is negative) about fiction. Once again the observant viewer is faced with brief glimpses of complex relationships which can make Vertov's work rich and frustrating in equal measure.

4.22.13	A movie poster – figures look left (like the man in painting).

At this point the viewer does not know which film the poster is advertising. The anchorage of the poster has been found and claimed by another film-maker (Vertov) to be utilized as an element in the diegesis of his own movie. In addition the viewer is now intrigued to know more about the poster.

4.26.01	Close-up of the woman in bed – the focus is woman's neckline.
4.29.08	Trees and tables at a windy coastal café. But where?
4.35.14	The woman is still in bed – the top of head, arm and the pattern on the bedspread all create a (retrospective) graphic match to the trees.
4.38.12	(Possibly) the same trees and a huge bottle.

Vertov could be creating a simple montage juxtaposition here. However the resonances are so rich that it seems more likely he is trying to represent a dream. Is this a criticism of the NEP dream – or an unmasking of the dream of fiction film? The answer is all of the above. This *is* a very complex film.

Vertov had tried to explain what we might think we are watching:

> You find yourself in a small but extraordinary land where all human experiences, behaviour and even natural phenomena are strictly controlled and occur at precisely determined times.
>
> ... If you wish, day will turn into night... According to your strict schedule people will fight and embrace, marry and divorce, are born and die, die and come to life.[10]

This is Vertov describing *fiction* film in the studio. Vertov wants to offer something else:

> High above this little fake world with its mercury lamps and electric suns, high in the real sky burns a real sun over real life, the Film Factory is a miniature island in the stormy sea of life.[11]

What the audience for *The Man with the Movie Camera* are about to see will include:

> Streets and street-cars intersect. So do buildings and buses, legs and smiling faces, hands and mouths, shoulders and eyes...
> A whirlpool of contacts, blows, embraces, games, accidents, athletics, dances, taxis, sights, thefts, incoming and outgoing papers set off against all sorts of seething human labour.[12]

Yuri Tsivian has noted that the opening is what you might expect from a fiction movie.[13] It is worth reiterating that Vertov is showing us what his film is not. He is playing games from the very start of the film. Even the 'city' of Vertov's symphony is itself more than a city. It is a 'virtual city' made up of fragments. Already Vertov and Svilova have utilized fragments of Moscow (the opening cityscape), Odessa (the windswept coast) and Kiev (the cinema).

4.42.12	A young man is asleep on a bench. His arm position exactly matches that of the woman. He does not move for 5.4 seconds.
4.47.20	A bin labelled 'keep it clean',
4.50.01	An urchin in rags,
4.51.18	Cut to close-up.
4.55.01	Straight cut to the 'Bakhmetiev Bus Depot' (Moscow).

The roof shape apes the position of the sleeper's arms and the split screen effects that will occur throughout the film.

4.58.10	Horse drawn carriages (without horses).

This shot appears to be an early example of the use of a wide-angle lens. Several planes of the image, including the rows of vehicles, are in focus.

5.02.20	A shop front – canted,
5.07.01	Roofs – matched on angle with the shop front,
5.10.23	Windows – also canted – followed by a shot of a courtyard that appears to be photographed looking down from a corner window.

Views of windows will remain a central visual element of the film. They take on the role of an icon (specific to *The Man with the Movie Camera*) that signifies looking. I choose that term rather than the more fashionable 'gaze' because Vertov's aim is scientific and his goal is complete transparency. All must look; all must be seen.

5.14.16	A graphic match with row of cots also at a canted angle.
5.18.22	A cross-fade to 5.19.12 – babies in split screen.

Next Vertov presents a brief hint of what is to come later in the film with a series of views: a window, a park, a kiosk, a park bench, mannequins, streets, shops, a mannequin apparently working a sewing machine and another riding a bicycle.

5.34.01   [1/12 point] The film's first shot of the Bolshoi Theatre:

The Bolshoi will reappear later in the film as an icon signifying (moribund) high culture. In this first appearance the theatre's dignity is undermined by an advertisement for Borzhomi mineral water which obscures part of its façade.

5.54.16   Another mannequin stares blankly into the camera lens.

However this inanimate image is given life by:

5.58.0	An eye-line match to cityscape – Tverskaia Street.
6.02.10	Mannequins in wig shop/hair salon.
6.05.08	A mannequin's eyes,
6.05.24	Matched to a building.
6.09.03	A mannequin behind a sewing machine.

This image is a reflection in a shop window that in itself reflects the activity occurring outside. By now the viewer may well now be questioning 'where is Dziga Vertov striding?'[14]

6.13.06   The corner of an apartment block – looking up in reversal of previous shot.

Vertov and Svilova are showing us they know the grammar of film: establishing shot, shot-reverse shot and so on. They are also showing us that these conventions do not, indeed cannot, tell the whole story.

6.36.00	Typewriter keyboard – close-up of keys.
6.38.01	[1/10 point] Full shot of typewriter.

Much as the cinema will replace the Bolshoi [1/12], so the typewriter [1/10] and other older forms of communication will be superseded by the moving image.

6.40.06   Fade up to a deserted street: Tverskaia Street, Moscow.

A further sequence constructed of seemingly unrelated inanimate objects unfolds. All these objects will reappear in action later in the film. The viewer is expected to notice and remember them.

7.34.02   A traffic signal is silhouetted against sky.

The action is about to start. Our point of view switches inside to a darkened hallway, looking out into the street through a glass door. A car – seen from above – arrives and the cameraman – his function signalled by his tripod – emerges and jumps into the car.

8.00.01   The cameraman strides towards the door and out
                       into the day.

The cameraman's car moves on. The cameraman – now revealed as Kaufman – begins his working day. Vertov had clearly warned his brother what to expect:

> A little man armed with a movie camera leaves the little fake world of the Film Factory and heads for life. Life tosses him here and there like a straw. He is like a frail canoe on a stormy sea. He is continually swamped by the furious traffic of the city. The rushing human crowd surges around him constantly. . . .
>
> Unlike the Film Factory, where the camera is almost stationary and where the whole of life is aimed at the camera's lens in a strictly determined order of shots and scenes, life here does not wait for the film director or obey the instructions.[15]

Episode 2: the cameraman's adventure

8.05.12   A film poster.

Members of the original audiences might have recognized the poster as advertising the melodrama *The Awakening of a Woman* [Das Erwachen des Weibes, Germany, 1927][16] which deals with sexual awakening. Many viewers may see this as a cue to a sexual reading of Vertov's film. There is certainly enough voyeuristic footage in the film to encourage such a reading. In any event *The Man with the Movie Camera* will not reveal the title of the German film until much later.

8.08.01   A high angle shot of a car moving along street left
                       to right.

8.11.06   Return to woman's head and arm – the pattern
                       echoes the curve of the road.

The Cine-Eyes – those most radical of film-makers – are once again showing very clearly that they know the rules of cinematography.

Having done so they can break or bend the rules with (knowledgeable) impunity.

8.13.14	Aerial shot: car turns corner (road closely matches woman's arm).
8.17.00	The car moves under an arch.
8.17.05	Cut to the car travelling under a bridge. The cameraman mounted. The shot is matched absolutely perfectly to the previous shot.
8.30.01	Pigeons take-off as if frightened by the car.

By this stage in the film it is impossible not to actively make connections between images. Vertov and Svilova make the viewer an accomplice in their project. So keen may the viewer be to 'decipher the world in a new way' that he or she may not notice that initially the pigeons are flying *backwards*.

In a reversal of the usual use of reverse action Svilova can then 'correct' the moving image to the forward moving one. This is only one of a multitude of occasions when *The Man with the Movie Camera* reveals the conventions of cinema by exposing them. The whole 'cameraman's adventure' episode apes the conventions of fiction film and the lessons of the 'Kuleshov effect' to *unmask* those conventions.

The cameraman begins his working day with some high-risk activity: filming trains from a railway track. Rapid pan shots eloquently illustrate the speed of the approaching train. These shots are inter-cut with close-ups of the cameraman's face and his foot snagging on the rail in a reference to classic scenes from adventure serials.

8.44.01	The car travels across left to right and exits at 8.47.24.
8.47.24	The sleeping woman's neck-line.
8.49.01	Seaside trees and tables.
8.52.08	Kaufman on a train track ... with a train approaching.

The train appears to get very close by 9.01.22. The mounted camera is on a track too and must be using a telephoto lens. Svilova executes some rapid inter-cutting including (from 9.18.03) black screen inserts of one to three frame duration. These inserts create a pulse rhythm.[17]

9.02.00	Tele-photo close-up of Kaufman's head as the train rushes past.
9.02.06	The side of the train travelling in the opposite screen direction.

9.03.01	Kaufman again – in reverse angle and screen direction.
9.03.11	The train as a blur and the action is reversed again.
9.03.08	A foot is caught on the rail.
9.04.22	Cuts to train from camera on the track – each shot has a different (canted) angle.
9.06.24	The woman's head/arm again: now she moves left to right.

Is the woman 'dreaming' the cameraman? Vlada Petrić[18] makes a strong case for the film's 'oneiric impact' particularly in this sequence. He concentrates on the formal aspects of graphic contrasts and montage intervals. Yet he fails to notice that the visual diegesis does intercut action and sleeping in a rather more direct way than he suggests.

Mikhail Kaufman steadfastly clung to a view of the Cine-Eyes as: 'intellectual engineers ... we were constructing thought out of figurative material.'[19] In this section at least Vertov does appear to be grappling rather crudely with a way to portray thought processes.

| 9.07.22 | The train hurtles past in exact reverse of the woman's head's movement. |

The images swing wildly in a movement very like a pendulum. The pendulum will return as a more overt image at the very end of the film.

9.11.20	A woman's head swings.
9.12.14	A train hurtles and swings past the camera.
9.13.18	A woman gets up.

The woman rouses herself. This particular edit is designed to produce a simple ideogram to signify 'attention'.

9.16.01	Train tracks [taken from train].
9.18.09	Black screen.
9.18.13	Shots of the track are inter-cut with black screen pulses.

The visual effect is also akin to blinking. This is an image that will occur again very shortly as a metaphor for photography.

| 9.23.01 | Kaufman emerges from his hole between the railway tracks. |

The significance of Kaufman's activity will be revealed in the Kiev station interlude [20.00.01].

This sequence ends with shots of the scenery and track 'passing' the train (shot from the train in what may be reference to the 'phantom rides' of early cinema). Kaufman jumps back. This action is part of the miraculous escape tradition but is also a joking referral to his brother's first film appearance jumping from a roof at Malyi Gnezdnikovsky Lane.[20] This is an example of Vertov's self-reference/compilation technique extending from his written to his filmed work.

In the following episode the cameraman leaves the railway line in his car. Presumably we should make a connection about 'progress and change' here. We watch Kaufman checking his equipment. Our attention is rather more taken by the intercut shots of the woman changing in a reverse strip tease.

Episode 3: 'Preparations'

9.30.24	The woman fastens her stockings.
9.35.18	Cut to the track. The car drives across right to left (a reverse) and exits the frame at 9.39.06.
9.40.08	Stockings – lingering on the process of fastening.
9.46.16	Pylons – Kaufman's car passes by.
9.49.20	Medium shot of the back of the woman (slightly irised). She removes her nightshirt and puts on her bra.

Seth Feldman writes of this sequence in 'Harmony of Man and Machine':

We get to the Cinema Eye through Life Caught Unawares, for one can only manipulate images by being true to their origins in the living world. In practice, the means of achieving life caught unawares varies. Those means could include what we would call 'candid camera'. We might, for instance, view the images of the woman getting dressed at the beginning of *The Man with the Movie Camera* as just such an invasion of privacy. But later in the film, when we discover that this woman is the editor, Svilova, Life Caught Unawares takes on another meaning. It is an agreement between the director and his subject that the camera has a right to be there.[21]

The problem is that – no matter how hard I try – I cannot see that this young, dark haired woman (seen in fuller face in the 'blinking' episode) *is* Svilova.

It being Svilova would certainly make sense in the diegesis. We have seen Kaufman go to work. We could, indeed should, see the editor. Why did Vertov *not* film his wife for this sequence? Vertov is constructing narratives and ideograms by connecting disparate material some of the time. At other times his construction is much more straightforward. Here is yet another puzzle for the viewer to be embroiled in.

Feldman points out that the people who are uncomfortable with the intrusion of the Cine-Eye: drunks, vagrants, 'NEP women', are the people whom Vertov is attacking in his film.

9.53.16	Detail of the fastening.
9.57.16	[3/20 point] Back to mid-shot of the fastening.

This sequence is surely also a metaphor for the construction of shot sequences in film.

9.59.01	The fastening.
9.59.17	Mid-shot: the woman puts on her shirt.
10.04.24	Cut to detail: Kaufman's camera.

This is *the* camera of the film's title. In a sequence to 10.10.04 a hand removes the standard lens (28 mm) and fits a telephoto lens. This is a clear visual cue. Now it is time to wake up. The whole tone and pace of the film changes from this point.

10.10.08	The camera is swung to side-on view.
10.10.23	A drunk is woken up. He rolls in the opposite screen direction.
	The camera swings. The drunk scratches himself.
10.17.12	Detail: the camera handle.
10.19.04	Head and shoulders shot of the drunk: he smiles.
	The camera swings away.
10.22.0	The camera is turning over (shot upside down).

This is a reference to the drunk's (mistaken) point of view. Vertov is constantly warning the viewer to beware and to observe closely and critically.

10.22.18	The drunk.
10.25.12	The camera turning over.
10.28.18	A Zeiss lens.

The lens holds a reflection of a camera turning over. This is the cameraman taking the shot the viewer is watching. The film moves on.

10.30.16	A woman sweeps the tram-lines.

Yuri Tsivian has explained the following sequence beautifully: '(For

Vertov) documentary works as wake-up therapy . . . the girl washes, the city washes . . . your life and the life of the city is one.'

10.36.18	Another sleeper awakes.
10.40.12	The lens.
10.42.18	The sleeper starts to rise.
10.48.02	Tverskaia Street again.

People are starting to appear on the street in a scene that does seem redolent of Ruttman. However, the German director was never as bold in his juxtaposition of images to create fuller meanings.

10.54.07	Detail: wash basin. A woman enters left to right.
11.01.06	The washing of the streets.

This juxtaposition may seem rather obvious. It is reasonable to assume that Vertov and Svilova made a deliberate decision to give the viewer *something* obvious at this point. Shots of various types of cleaning continue:

11.05.01	[1/6 point] A close-up of the hosing down of street lamps.
11.06.00	A woman is washing.
11.11.08	Washing the bin (already seen 4.47.20).

Here Vertov is reusing images to give them retrospective meaning. This is a ploy that occurs throughout the film. Viewers should be constantly aware of, and looking for, this technique. Awareness will invariably explain the appearance of elements that initially seem puzzling or irrelevant. Close observation of when and how these reappearances occur give strong hints as to political meanings in the film.

11.17.00	The woman is towelling herself.
11.21.20	Window cleaning: the female window cleaner looks down.
11.26.09	The woman is towelling her face.

All this sweeping and washing, coming as it does at a 1/6th point, must have a meaning. We are seeing a cleansing, or to use the Russian term to clean: *chistit* . The term *chistka* was used to signify a political purge. The first 'purge' of the communist Party had taken place in 1921 to enforce discipline during NEP. The next took place before and during the Fifteenth Party Congress of 1927.[22] Vertov's own pronouncements, from 'We' onwards, suggest cinema needs cleansing of old bourgeois narratives. *The Man with the Movie Camera* clearly endorses the invigorating character of rigorous sweepings. As such the film can serve as an illustration of the atmosphere which Stalin could use in his purgings of the 1930s. *The Man with the Movie Camera* can be seen as an early example of 'Stalinist' cinema, coming as it does from the most eloquent work of a politically committed film-maker working at exactly the moment when the new order was about to assert itself. Having made a clear political point, Vertov returns to his exposition on the nature of cinema.

11.30.19	Eyes open.
11.30.22	Shutters open.
11.33.12	A lens pull.

Flowers are shown going in and out of focus. This may not be particularly subtle juxtaposition but it is a simple, and witty, primer in basic photography. The woman blinks again and the camera irises. These actions are closely matched.

11.43.00	The shutters close, open and close – intercut with:
11.47. 53	(Washing) woman's eyes blinking.
11.53.08	The lens: aperture closed down and opened.

We have been shown how photography works. In the film's second reel we will see the technology – and Kaufman – in action.

Episode 4: The camera in action

12.00.16	The second reel starts with a mobile shot under trees.
12.03.14	The screen is practically black.

The cameraman emerges into light to reveal reality that can look like photographic effects and *vice versa*. The mobile camera is approaching a building.

12.12.20	Cut to the span of a bridge – Kaufman mounting – silhouetted.

The frame is canted. Kaufman sets up his camera.

12.19.12	The shed gates rise to reveal aeroplanes.
12.30.01	The planes are brought forward.
12.37.20	Cut to tramway point – being oiled – the cross is at the centre point of the frame.
12.43.01	The trams emerge.

This could be a telephoto but is quickly (12.43.24) revealed as a super-imposition.

12.48.01	Actuality – as the trams are lined up in what *looks* like a superimposition.

12.50.22	Kaufman strides along the support of a bridge.
12.53.01	A tram passes.

The passenger leaning out of the window is Dziga Vertov. This is a joke within the film. It is also a jokey reference to an earlier Vertov film *Kinopravda* 3. In this film coverage of the trial of the Socialist Revolutionaries was refreshed by a shot of Vertov and his brother emerging from a cab to buy a paper.

12.58.09	The Bakhmetiev Park bus garage.

The roof of the garage actually looks like a split-screen image.
Buses emerge and at:

13.08.01	A swing past the camera following a line set by pedestrians.
13.16.01	[1/5 point] Buses pass the garage.
13.21.01	Cut to a poster for the film *The Sold Appetite* [Prodannyi appetit, 1928] which features a bus.

Apart from the obvious visual connection to the preceding shot, the reference to this contemporary Soviet film has a political point to make. Nikolai Okhlopov's film was 'a social satire on millionaires' and as such was a criticism of urban decadence. *The Man with the Movie Camera* extends the criticism with its next shot.

13.24.08	A tram moves behind woman asleep on bench.
13.28.08	An eye is superimposed on a Zeiss lens. It is possible to see clearly the hand cranking. The eye line swings left-to-right and is matched to:
13.29.08	Woman's legs.
13.31.12	The lens/eye winks and swings right-to-left matched on action to:
13.35.01	the woman indignantly rises and is out of frame at 13.35.18
13.36.08	Long shot of a city corner – trams intersect.
13.44.01	The window of the Gostorg offices in Moscow filmed at eye level with the street movement reflected.
13.51.01	The path of the tram curves up and left-to-right (filmed from above).
14.00.01	Kaufman strides past a cinema showing *The Awakening of a Woman*.

Connections are being made. It is reasonable to suggest that the observations in this sequence are about the phenomenon of making connections. Yuri Tsivian sees Kaufman walk past the poster (the cinema of dreams) and into the chaos of life. Tsivian cannot resist seeing Kaufman as 'Buster Keaton'. He also notes that the eye in the lens is Vertov's. In later sequences it will be Svilova's.

| 14.03.20 | Long shot of a tram. |
| 14.10.01 | The camera follows and takes up the movement of the tram. |

This is a genuinely exciting moment as the 'viewer' is taken up in the momentum of the action. We are now part of the film's diegesis.

Vertov presents another one of his 'industrial process' sequences (as featured in *One Sixth of the World* and *The Eleventh Year*). Machines work, a mine lift operates and men or horses pull mine carts. Kaufman is seen lying on the ground filming these carts in the same way as he filmed the train. Kaufman begins a – risky looking – ascent up a huge chimney.

Yuri Tsivian has pointed out that the shots of chimneys and smoke were photographed thousands of miles away from those of the miners digging coal which follow immediately. He asks, perhaps facetiously, if this is a lesson in Marxist political economy. Annette Michelson has put the case that this and many other sequences in *The Man with the Movie Camera* are precisely that.[23]

This sequence also leads Tsivian to discuss the concepts of 'life as it is' and 'life caught unawares'. The shots of city and working life seem entirely apposite for such a discussion. Tsivian warns us to be careful in distinguishing the two: 'not synonymous'.

'Life as it is' involves the registering of events exactly as they would happen when you were not registering them. Vertov and his critics were aware of how difficult that was. Vertov and Kaufman thought long and hard about techniques to get around the problem of people's reactions to filming. The use of telephoto lens was one tactic. Kaufman is seen changing to telephoto early in the film. However, in 1929 a telephoto lens could only be used outdoors and in good light. The hidden camera was a possibility and can be seen in this sequence. Kaufman often used a noisy and obvious dummy whilst filming with a smaller more discreet camera.

Vertov preferred a more all-encompassing method. People had to be made used to cameras rattling away on every street corner. This totalitarian fantasy has only become a possibility in recent years with the advent of CCTV. Again history has shown Vertov to be a visionary and a political *naif*. Kaufman was against this fantasy: his preferred approach was to train ordinary people in non-acting. Shklovsky, never slow to see an open door for criticism, likened 'trying to teach the whole population of the Soviet Union to act' to 'hammering the wall into the nail.'[24] A completely different approach would be to 'catch life unawares' by allowing people to react, even provoking them to do so.

From 14.30.01 Kaufman goes about the business of 'capturing life' both as it is and 'unawares'. His work includes the long ascent of a factory chimney whilst encumbered by a Debrie camera.

16.29.14	Buses travel right to left.
16.34.12	Kaufman moves away from camera on scaffold.
16.37.01	[1/4 point] Kaufman minces down the gantry before the voyage into 'the market'.

Kaufman's walk is a parody of a woman's gait. He appears to be followed by two women – filmed from behind – chatting as they walk along a street.

16.45.01	The camera follows the women.
16.48.24	A street market opens.

The camera swings in the opposite direction to the incoming crowds. This movement echoes and reverses the earlier tram shot [14.10.01]. The market shots are the only item in the film in which the countryside comes to the city. This short sequence is the only example of the 'link' (*smychka*) between the city and the countryside that had been so central to Vertov's earlier work.

The Man with the Movie Camera is a film about links and 'connections' but the *smychka* has been broken. The behaviour of the traders is seen in stark contrast to the disciplined (and clean) workers who dominate the film. The countryside comes to the town as an uncontrollable mob. Thus Vertov's film can be seen as an indicator of the change of mood amongst (urban) Bolshevik supporters which would lend support to Stalin's declaration of war against the peasants in 1928–29. *The Man with the Movie Camera* can be viewed as a manifesto for Stalin's policies of the 1930s: crush resistance in the countryside, urbanize, industrialize and purge opposition. One of the forces Stalin was determined to crush was the market. In *The Man with the Movie Camera* the market symbolizes both the countryside and the market system of NEP.

The gates of a large outdoor market open and the stall-holders run in with their goods to gain a good pitch. The cameraman, apparently caught unawares himself, is now amongst the crowd. The market scenes are filmed with a telephoto lens to achieve an effect of exaggerated tightness and speed of action.

17.27.12	A tram passes left to right:
17.33.01	To reveal (very briefly) the traffic signal at a road junction.

This signal will take on iconographic significance during the film.

17.33.10	Stall-holders hang dresses at the market.
17.36.09	A woman checks eggs.
17.39.10	A high shot of a wide avenue – a tram crosses right to left exactly mid-way through the shot.

This street scene is filmed from the roof-tops to give an effect of omniscience.

17.45.01	The tram's left-right movement is matched by movement of a window opening into the camera plane.

A window opening is used again as a cue for a scene of the private realm.

17.46.16	Teeth are cleaned left to right, up and down.
17.49.08	The shutters are removed from a food store (*gastronom*).

From the orthography we can see this is Russia not the Ukraine.

17.53.08	A post box.
17.57.14	The store front.
18.03.10	Mid-shot of the traffic signals – the traffic policeman turns the axis of the signal towards the camera, cut to:
18.06.10	Shutters rise to reveal an advertisement for a tour on a passenger ship named 'LENIN'.

The trip is from Odessa to Yalta. The audience will be involved in this trip and activity at the coastal resort later in the film.

18.10.12	Another busy street corner.
18.22.05	A fountain in front of the Bolshoi Theatre, Moscow.
18.24.12	Mid-shot of the fountain.
18.32.18	A black transition to the shutters, followed by:

Stop-action/overlapping one second shots of shutters opening. The sequence shows the shutters from the front, from the right and from left before repeating the front view from a closer vantage point. The Cine-Eye is exploring and getting closer.

The Cine-Eye can reveal different aspects of the same action in a way reminiscent of a Cubist painting. The difference is that in cinema we can see each aspect clearly as well as simultaneously. The Cine-Eye also allows time to be stretched as well as elided.

18.36.06	A mannequin 'operates' a sewing machine.

The illusion of the mannequin sewing reveals how easily the viewer can be tricked. This shot is cut to another shop shutter.

18.40.20	The shutter rises to reveal an advertisement for spectacles.

The verbal joke plays on the Russian word for spectacles (*ochki*) as yet another reference to Vertov's team (*kinoki*). It is part of a visual joke about the unreliability of eyesight that is also by extension an affirmation of the superiority of the Cine-Eye.

A pan shot reveals a shop front which acts as a mirror. We catch a glimpse of the film poster, the cameraman himself (filming) and the street behind.

18.53.22	A mannequin is (apparently) bicycling.

Reflections of the world 'caught unawares' in the window are visible to the cameraman and thus the viewer.

19.03.20	A post bike travels left to right.
19.08.12	At the crossroads the policeman gives directions.
19.13.12	The post bike – the camera dollies in and pans left-right to:
19.17.01	The roof of a train (curving right-left).
	A tram travels right-left out of shot.
19.29.01	Trams travel either side of camera (which is positioned between the tracks).
19.31.10	A telephoto shot of a train carriage travelling right to left.

Is the train speeding up or is this a camera trick? Vertov will not let the viewer relax for one second. *The Man with the Movie Camera* keeps asking questions and demanding close attention. The train shot is cut jarringly to:

19.35.01	Split screen images of a street form a V pattern on the screen.

On both axes of the split image the camera moves in the same direction but the people move in opposite directions. This composite image is a reference to the previous reflection shots and a splendid metaphor for the complexity of 'life as it is.'

19.39.16   A camera placed above Kaufman films him filming on the side of a speeding train.

19.54.01   [6/20 point] is the point at which the train passes over the camera.

The viewer saw Kaufman place the camera on the tracks earlier [9.23.01]. Increasingly we are being asked to understand life by piecing together information we are receiving with information we have already received. The whole film is now clearly signalled as an educative process that needs to be worked at by looking, learning and utilizing previous experience. The lessons do not have to be dull or dry, as Vertov and Svilova demonstrate in the next 'episode'.

Episode 5: 'The chase (life caught unawares)'

20.00.01   The train comes to a complete halt.

20.02.01   Cut to a crowd at the Central Station, Kiev.

This scene is a continuation of the film's theme of connections. It must also be a homage to the Lumière brothers' *L'Arrivée du train en gare* [France, 1895] and therefore a comment on and tribute to the history of cinema.

20.06.01   Horse-drawn cabs circle outside the station.

20.13.01   Kaufman films from his car.

A dispassionate observer may ask (and will ask again during later sequences) why no other cameraman was credited for this film.

20.15.01   Kaufman focuses on one cab.

20.17.01   The shot is matched to a similar shot of Kaufman's car.

Kaufman's pursuit of two cabs is cross-cut with the departure of the train. The movement of the train's wheels is cross-cut and matched with the movements of the cameraman's arm. The chase sequence would remind contemporary viewers of American films. Vertov had not abandoned his attraction to them as expressed in 'We': 'To the American adventure film with its showy dynamism ... the Cine-Eyes say thanks for the rapid shot changes and the close-up.'[25] Even a chase sequence must serve multiple purposes for Vertov.

21.33.01   In the 'well dressed' cab the woman passenger apes
                  Kaufman's camera cranking.
This shot allows Vertov to remind the viewer of the filming process. It
also allows Svilova to contrast the unconcerned 'natural' reactions of
the travellers in the crowded cab with the self-conscious behaviour of
two evidently well-to-do women.

Episode 6: 'Process'
The viewer has already seen how film is exhibited (prologue) and
filmed (the cameraman's adventures). Now Vertov and Svilova treat us
to an inside look at the process of editing.

21.53.01   A shot of a cab horse running is brought to a
                  STILL at 21.55.12.
21.57.01   A still of a woman (with an umbrella).
22.02.01   A still of the street (from the previous 'V' section).
22.04.00   A still of the women in the cab.
22.09.01   [1/3 point] A still: long shot (high angle) of a main
                  street.
At this pivotal moment of the film Vertov chooses to show us the city
stilled by the power of the cinema i.e. the moving picture can be used
to *stop* action in order to decode it. It is important to remember that
this godlike action was taken by the director and executed by the editor
not 'the man with the movie camera', however much Kaufman might
protest.

The sequence continues with stills of an old woman and moving
pictures of a little girl. These shots were featured in a sequence entitled:
'How the Chinese magician Xhan Ti Xhan earns his bread' from *The
Cine-Eye* [1924]. That sequence in *The Cine-Eye* begins with the
magician striding out to begin his day's work in a way very reminiscent
of Kaufman in *The Man with the Movie Camera*.

Sections of *The Man with the Movie Camera* which have already been
projected – including the mine and the women in the carriage – are
seen labelled and hanging in Svilova's editing room. Svilova is 'caught
unawares' organizing material labelled: 'Traffic', 'city', 'factory',
'machines', 'bazaar' and 'magician'. Svilova brings bits of film – a
small boy laughing, the little girl and the woman with the scarf 'back
to life'. This process will be examined several times in the film. As
Vertov put it himself:

Note: A small, secondary production theme – the film's passage from camera through laboratory and editing room to screen – will be included, by montage, in the film's beginning, middle, and end.[26]

22.13.01	A still of a woman's head (taken from the market shots) is cut to:
22.17.15	A strip of film (of a smiling girl).

This is a rather imaginative presentation of a '*moving* image' – i.e. the actual film which produces that image – as a *still* image.

22.23.03	A still of a young woman with scarf is cut to a repetition of:
22.27.10	A strip of film (smiling girl).
22.32.06	Strips of film are back-lit on hangers.
22.38.20	Reels of film are labelled: 'factory', 'machines', 'market'.
22.40.21	Detail: shot of an editing table (a winding spool) cut to:
22.43.05	Another still of a film-strip (young woman with a white scarf).
22.46. 01	A stop-action sequence shows the spool taking up film.
22.49.01	Svilova is spooling film at her editing table.

Vertov moves from presentation of the abstract activity (using the technology of cinema) to a showing of the actual activity. That the activity is in itself part of film-making makes the whole sequence more interesting.

22.52.01	Film is moving on a light board. (Scissors enter the frame at 22.55.22)
22.57.01	Svilova cuts and pastes film.
23.00.01	A still of the woman in white scarf.
23.02.23	Svilova works at her film bank.
23.07.01	The woman in white scarf is now set in motion.
23.10.18	Svilova works at her light board.
23.12.12	Another still – an Agfa film strip of laughing children (taken from *The Cine-Eye*).
23.13. 01	[7/20 point] A still of a little boy on a film strip.

This charming still (placed at a significant sectioning point) is followed by a crucial and wonderful moment in the film as at 23.16.16 the film comes to life. Pictures are made to move.

23.20.22	Svilova continues to work magic at her light board.
23.23.01	A still of more images of laughing children (from *The Cine-Eye*) on a film strip.
23.27.01	The film 'comes to life.'
23.31.10	Still of the old woman from the market.
23.32.00	Still of the street panorama.
23.33.12	The children as a moving image.
23.35.01	The street panorama as a moving image.
23.40.08	The old woman argues (in close up) with the camera.
23.45.01	Svilova.
23.46.01	Film moves over a light board and comes to a stop at:
23.47.18	Still frames of a new born baby.
23.48.08	A still of the women in the cab with the umbrella is brought to life at 23.50.01

By now Vertov can effortlessly suggest that it is the very process of filming and editing that brings life. He can return to more ostensibly political manipulation of images. The female cab passengers from the Kiev chase scene are shown disembarking from the carriage. Servants carry their luggage. The viewer is invited, if not required, to disapprove of the vestiges of NEP.

Episode 7: 'Life caught unawares' (general)
The cameraman continues his progress. The life of the city goes on around him. People rush through a revolving door.

24 34.12	Revolving doors.
24.37.20	A panorama of a city square.
24.44.01	Straight shot of revolving door: people are coming in and past the camera.
24.50.22	High shot of a corner: traffic.

A woman speaks on a telephone. The policeman is still on traffic duty. The movement of the camera matches the movement of his signal. The camera lens swings down to photograph the city.

In the registry office one couple (boldly) marry and another couple (more furtively) get divorced. A traffic signal directs the camera to swing 180° from one couple to the other. The married couple are photographed together as the divorced couple are until the image splits them in close ups. The street once again folds into a "V" and the tram goes around a corner.

26.39.01	[8/20 point] The trams cross.
26.43.18	Cut to another divorcing couple.

The woman in the registry office hides her face and is cross-cut to:

26.47.01	A woman crying at a graveside.
26.51.00	Divorcing couple: the woman hides her face as the man laughs.
26.57.13	A crying woman is prostrate on the ground.
27.03.01	Divorcing couple: she leaves as he signs.

Vertov now crosscuts a wedding, a funeral and a woman giving birth.

27.40.01	[approaching and through the 5/12 point] A mother in childbirth.
27.49.01	A funeral cortège passes.
27.59.20	The child emerges and the cord is unwrapped.

All human life is here in its glorious confusion as given sense by *The Man with the Movie Camera*. As the funeral ends a baby is born, washed and given to its mother.

Tsivian describes reel three as 'about highly organized life' and notes how the camera is imperious in its approach to so many activities including birth and death. The more interventionist activity of the editor allows the camera to appear to be assisting in the birth. Immediately after the baby emerges [28.03.01] Svilova cuts to a shot of Kaufman filming superimposed over 'v' of split-screen buildings which echoes the mother's legs.

At 28.27.01 the camera is back between trams (going both back and forward). Shots of speeded up trams are intercut with a lift coming down and its passengers emerging into the hallway featured in the first reel. At the end of this sequence Vertov and his team play a trick on the viewer. First we are shown a shot – presumably taken by Kaufman – from the lift but what we see is Kaufman filming the lift. When we reach a higher floor he is filming 'us' again.

To extend the 'tricks' sequence Vertov constructs complex shots where bits of the frame are filled with different images. This allows trams to 'crash' and vehicles to scatter crowds as images converge and diverge. Rapid pans produce a feeling of motion but also confusion.

29.57.12	[9/20 point] A tram passes over the camera.

There follows a breathtaking piece of montage on the theme of seeing:

29.58.03	Five frames of black then 2 frames of sky introduces 'the Cine-Eye'.
29.58.11	An eye (it is Svilova's) to 29.58.14 (i.e just three frames).
29.58.16	A street panorama (whip pan).
29.59.17	The eye (seven frames).
29.59.24	The street (with a wildly swinging panning camera).
30.00.01	The eye matched to the panorama.
30.01.02	The street cobbles – the camera swings up to the street scene.
30.01,21	The eye (three frames).
30.02.01	The street (swinging camera).
30.02.21	The eye (two frames), cut to the street.
30.03.23	The eye (two frames) matched to a whip-pan panorama from the rooftops past the bus station.
30.05.07	The eye.

The corner of the square tilted at 90 degrees.

30.06.07	The eye followed by a panorama of roof tops,
30.07.07	The eye.
30.07.15	Horses – head on.
30.08.07	The eye.

The visual effect of blinking is underpinned by a motor rhythm created by changing the duration of the 'eye' shots. The much bigger pans and tracks of the cut-aways match slight movements of the iris.

30.16.23–24   A whip pan of the street scene.

The image of eye is superimposed over the initial frame of the 2–3 frame shots of the street scene. At 30.18.22 Vertov inserts a single frame shot of the eye.

Svilova's eye/city panorama shots are indeed reduced to single frame duration. Svilova holds this stream of images together and gives it a sense of rhythm by utilizing some double exposure. The sense of overwhelming speed is achieved by running the film at 24 frames per second. This effect is in itself further proof that the film works best at this projection speed.

The camera eye blinks. A woman talks on the phone.

Episode 8: 'Life caught unawares' (the particular)

30.18.23	A woman talks on the phone (close-up, canted angle).
30.20.01	An ambulance, the crew boards and the vehicle exits the frame.
30.26.01	An ambulance passes over camera (echoing shots of the train and the tram in previous episodes) before a return to the woman on the phone.

The phone-call (for help?) cuts to a neat cinematic joke. Svilova's montage makes it appear the caller then warns the Cine-Eye HQ. Kaufman sets off in hot pursuit. *The Man with the Movie Camera* has returned to melodrama.

30.28.01	Kaufman jumps into his car.
30.34.11	The phone is hung up.

In a moment of (genuine) 'life caught unawares' the phone misses its cradle at the first attempt.

Throughout the 'emergency' the viewer is watching Kaufman. 'The man with the movie camera' is an actor in this whole episode. We are reminded that he is after all the star of the film rather than its creator. This is Vertov's film and a tribute to Svilova's skills.

30.36.01	Kaufman follows the ambulance.

This shot consists of a *very* smooth pan that suggests it was rehearsed.

30.43.20	Close-up of the head injury.

The camera is hand-held and its subject is moved in and out of frame. The following sequence is made up of simple shot-reverse shots which produce the illusion of a chase between the ambulance and the fire engine.

32.16.01	Tracking shot of fire engine (with cameraman in full view).

The camera pulls back to reveal the cameraman mounted on the engine. It is *not* Kaufman. This shot allows us to:

(a) appreciate a Vertovian joke – he had fooled us into thinking Kaufman was acting not filming at all in this episode. Then he cuts in a sequence that was filmed by Kaufman.

(b) identify the other (uncredited) 'man with the movie camera'. Reference to earlier group shots of the Cine-Eye group identifies him as Peter Zotov.

32.20.20	The film's second unit performs a tracking shot of the fire engine.

| 32.32.17 | The camera (with telephoto lens) tilts up to reveal reflection of another camera in its lens. |

The fourth reel begins with this literally reflexive image of a camera reflected in the lens of another camera. After travelling shot past tall buildings, we see Kaufman setting up a shot of the traffic signal. A brief shot of the divorcing woman [32.46.02 to 32.48.01] introduces a sequence of women being shampooed and manicured

Episode 9: Midpoint/political comparisons

32.48.01	A close-up of woman being made-up: eyes.
32.50.08	The divorcing woman *covers* her eyes.
32.51.13	A woman being made up (smiling).
32.53.05	A working woman slapping mortar on to a wall (mid-shot).
33.00.07	The eye is made up.
33.02.07	The working woman turns to the camera then carries on working.

Vertov and Svilova are making a political point through editing. This simple juxtaposition manages to praise honest toil and criticize NEP at the same time. In addition they can both underline and humanize their point by allowing their subjects to 'perform' before the camera e.g.:

33.07.15	The working woman plays coyly to the camera.
33.11.01	Washing hair.
33.11.01	Washing curtains.

This shot carries on through *the mid-point of the film* [33.15]. Why is this apparently inconsequential activity positioned at the very mid-point of this film? The answer is that in a film so carefully constructed nothing is inconsequential. This washing and cleansing sequence coming after the juxtaposition of working woman and the beauty parlour creates a message: purge (*chistit'*)

33.16.21	Washing hair – head revealed.
33.20.09	Washing curtains.
33.23.15	Washing hair.
33.26.21	Wringing the curtains.
33.30.08	Lathering for shaving.
33.32.13	A razor being sharpened on a strap.
33.36.01	Shaving.

This shot leads to a rather more chilling 'cut':

| 33.37.22 | An axe is sharpened. |

33.41.01   Hair drying: close-up of a woman's head.

Is Vertov suggesting off with her head? The movement of the drier is matched to:

33.44.01   A hand cranking a camera – matched back to a head turning.

This shot constitutes a graphic match with a one-frame superimposition for a transition to:

33.49.05   A sign for 'expert shoeshine from Paris'.

The camera can be seen as a reflection in the sign. Once again the operator is not Kaufman. The man in the cap is Zotov.

33.54.01   Shoe shining.

33.58.01   Hair cutting (back of woman's head).

34.01.01   A mid-shot of a manicure (the same woman).

34.04.01   The haircut is in progress.

34.06,01   A close-up of the manicure of equipment and hands is matched to:

34.08.11   Svilova pasting film.

34.12.01   Manicure.

34.14.01   Film is spliced (cut-away to paste).

34.18.01   Manicure.

34.21.01   A mid-shot of a woman sewing is cut-away to a close-up of (her?) face and hands.

34.28.18   A lens is focused.

34.30.01   A hand cranks a camera.

34.31.06   Woman/sewing machine – cutaways to hands and handles, strips being sewn.

34.40.01   Film is spooled across a light box.

This shot is matched to:

34.43.01   A sewing machine wheel. The operator's hand movement (left to right) is matched to:

34.46.01   Svilova reaching for film strips (right to left).

34.49.21   Svilova's hand-written markers.

34.52.01   A woman's head turns, as do the wheels of machinery.

34.56.21   Svilova arranges clips.

34.57.23   Woman and machine.

There is a whip-pan back and forth to the machinist's work-mate and down to her machine. This device achieves a sense of equivalence between operator and machine.

Yuri Tsivian has noted how the cuts/contrasts juxtapose service (heads) and production (hands). Production is good and film-making is included in the production shots. The direct comparison of film-making and shining shoes is an ironic reference to Vertov's 1923 attack on fiction film-makers as 'the shoe-shiners'.[27] The juxtaposition of manicure and film splicing go beyond a visual reference. Both activities use acetone. Thus Vertov is cross-cutting and matching by smell.

Tsivian also suggests that the 'production' shots which follow are a precursor to Vertov's first sound film *Enthusiasm*. They are certainly redolent of the atmosphere of the Soviet Union about to enter the first Five Year Plan.

As Seth Feldman puts it:

In keeping with the notion of the film-maker as nothing more than another worker, *The Man with the Movie Camera* offers us a recurring visual metaphor for the editor, that of the traffic cop at the busy intersection. It is she who controls the flow of film images (just as the film stock itself is compared visually to a rapidly passing railroad track seen from above). And it is also her editing that bridges the concepts of Life Caught Unawares and the Cinema Eye.[28]

35.05.18   The traffic policeman turns his signal.
This is a signal for a change in subject matter. The productionist theme continues.

Episode 10: Labour of man and machine, man-machine
35.09.05   An abacus is placed alongside a sign: 'observe
                    silence'.
This dual image signals both that the next sequence has a theme of calculation and the audience's need for careful attention.
35.14.13   A cigarette (*papirosa*) packet machine.
35.20.17   A cash till.
The hand cranking the till echoes the action of a camera operator and matches (in opposition) the actions of the cigarette machine.
35.24.14   Newspapers.
35.28.01   A woman's hands making packets matched on
                    action to:
35.31.01   The same woman's head and shoulders.
The cutting between the two images is speeding up as the head-shot

gets tighter and tighter. The final close up has the head positioned down to allow an eye-line match to the packing machine.

A young woman is talking off camera. She clearly knows she is on camera but is unconcerned. She symbolizes the open honesty of the Soviet worker whilst embodying exactly the type of subject Vertov's method cried out for.

35.57.15	Hands operate a switchboard at a furious pace.
36.03.09	The operators are shown in mid-shot.
36.07.01	The switchboard.
36.11.13	(Disembodied) hands pack cigarettes.

From 36.16.16 the activity of cigarette packing is inter-cut with a wider shot of the switchboard operators. The images are under-cranked and shortened in duration – and painstakingly matched – until Vertov arrives at a lightning montage of shots as short as two frames.

| 36.33.18 | [11/20 point] A cut from the cigarettes to the switchboard cues a further shortening of shot length. |

The montage continues to accelerate.

| 36.36.12 | The montage reaches the speed of two frame shots. |
| 36.38.18 | The typewriter keyboard. |

The feverish typing appears to write a series of images mostly of hands *doing* things: cranking a camera, a three frame shot [at 35.46.09] of a hand raising a gun, plugging in an electric lead, hanging up a phone, sharpening an axe. These images have, apart from the gun, been seen earlier in the film. Now they become a frenzied blur until Svilova arrives to make sense of the world the camera has 'caught unawares':

| 37.02.01 | Svilova enters. |

Svilova's hands organize Kaufman's rushes. The editing room sequence cuts to footage of Kaufman filming in a mine.

38.01.12	Svilova organizes rushes.
38.05.12	Kaufman enters a steel mill and films the metal smelting.
38.47.01	[7/12 point] The camera tracks to a close-up of the furnace.

The cameraman films and the editor edits the shots. Spindles in motion are inter-cut and matched to water pouring over a dam. The dam is the most potent symbol of Soviet power embodying the ability to build huge structures and to produce electricity. This shot taken from *The Eleventh Year* allows Vertov to make a very direct connection between construction and the power needed to drive the new mechanized Soviet Union. All activity is connected. All activity is necessary. That which is not – i.e. the fripperies of NEP – will be washed away (*chistit*). The water in the dam can serve as a metaphor for the political as well as the economic point.

39.54.01   [12/20 point] The dam.

Kaufman rises up suspended by a crane. Kaufman is suspended above the dam. Shots of Kaufman filming the dam are inter-cut with machinery in motion.

40.50.06   Kaufman and his assistant suspended over the dam.

40.55.19   A split screen (top/bottom) is constructed from images of trams.

Once again the screen splits to allow us to see multiple images of city life. The very rapid montage inter-cuts cameraman and machinery. Juxtapositions – including split screens – match circular movements of camera and machinery.

41.18.01   A matched shot of a camera (over) cranking.

The *editor* creates this effect rather than the cameraman.

The shot lengths shorten. A series of single frame shots produce an effect of Kaufman carrying camera superimposed over an industrial landscape. He turns towards 'our' camera.

41.38.15   A one-frame superimposition of a lens cut to the traffic policeman. This time the camera is evidently on a moving vehicle passing him.

41.38.16   The traffic point.

The camera moves past at normal speed but its progress feels like slow motion due to the previous sequence. The Cine-Eye can alter the perception of time.

41.44.21   A tracking shot of car passing the traffic point left-to-right.

41.50.09   Detail of a car horn.

41.51.11   Traffic moves past the check point in the opposite direction.

Kaufman is on the ground filming the shot we have already seen. [35.05.18]

Shots of Kaufman filming in the middle of the road and the car hurtling along are cross-cut. A hand squeezes the horn of the car.

41.59.11   Kaufman strides towards the camera carrying *his* camera and sets up a shot.

This process is interspersed with cut-aways of the car horn.

42.02.11   Kaufman is filming between trams towards the viewers' point of view shot from behind Kaufman.

42.11.21   The 'split screen' of trams.

42.14.18   The lens pans down.

42.19.07   The machines stop.

Episode 11: Rest

At the start of reel five the camera is stopping machinery. The workers seen earlier in the film now groom themselves.

43.00.03   Trees sway in the wind [a repeat of the shot at 04.29.08].

43.05.14   A boat moves past the camera.

For a moment it is unclear if the boat *is* moving or if we are watching a pan shot.

43.13.01   [13/20 point] the camera begins to pan up

A banner is revealed: 'The struggle for peace involves the whole Soviet land.'

43.30.22   The beach.

Tsivian has noted how Odessa beach is brought to Moscow right on time for the end of the working day. Kaufman's camera cruises the beach taking particular interest in young women. Reel four had worshipped the machine. Reel five will take a closer interest in bodies. Simple 'rest' cannot be allowed to continue for long. All time must be used productively.

Episode 12: Recreation

44.11.22   An open space:

44.15.01   Exercisers are faded into the frame.

44.18.12   A magician's paraphernalia:

44.21.02   [2/3 point] The magician fades in.

The Cine-Eye will now do its own magic.

44.25.01   Water:

44.26.01   Slow fade in of swimmers.

44.35.01   A covered fairground ride:

44.35.01	A fade in reveals the fairground horses beneath their cover.
44.44.01	A miniature tower is 'constructed' in stop-action.
44.53.01	A wall newspaper is constructed.

The newspaper is from Odessa film studio. It includes a *Kul't-anketa* (a culture-questionnaire), which the film answers itself.

| 45.21.06 | The camera picks out an article 'about sport.' |

This is the cue for the sporting section of the film. The viewer is sure to be reminded of the long-heard call of the socialist movement (central to Trotsky's article about the uses of cinema) for eight hours rest, eight hours work and eight hours leisure. Naturally the thrust of the film's argument is that leisure should be used constructively.

| 45.23.22 | A discus thrower performs in slow motion. |

This shot leads to a sequence of athletes engaged in a wide range of activities from discus and hammer throwing to hurdling (including stop-action) and volleyball.

| 46.32.01 | [14/20 point] The first cross-cut between viewer/ volleyball game. |

The athletes perform in slow motion while spectators look on in standard speed footage. Tsivian memorably describes Vertov's use of slow motion as a 'close-up of time.' He also notes that the action is eroticized by the cut-aways to spectators. I would add that this occurs many times in the film not just in the overtly sexualized sporting/ dancing sequences. Women on the beach apply mud or cosmetics to themselves. Vertov continues his exploration of eroticized body parts.[29] Women lie and stretch sleepily.

Masses of people disembark from the boat for their turn at this paradise of self-improvement. Amongst the crowd is Kaufman.

49.01.12	Kaufman strides down the gangplank (with his camera).
49.33.12	Kaufman takes his camera for a tour of the beach.
49.55.14	[3/4 point] Kaufman is in sea with his camera.
50.08.12	A head and shoulders shot of a young man.

Is he observing the activity on the beach? Vertov and Svilova can use this cinematic puzzle to link to the next episode with an eye-line match.

Episode 13: Sport

| 50.10.05 | A magician performs. |

The viewer now watches a sequence from *The Cine-Eye*. The viewer will already have seen Svilova edit this sequence and literally give it life [23.12.12]. Surely the central point of *The Man with the Movie Camera* is that editing/organizing material is the key to the Cine-Eye process. The magician performs his tricks. Clearly prestidigitation is seen as akin (or at least parallel) to editing.

The beautiful little girl in the magician's audience stares questioningly and by another eye-line match leads the viewer to an apparently unconnected sequence of body-building. It is worthy of note that many of these images are also heavily eroticized, e.g.

50.54.12   A woman exercises on a rowing machine with the camera's focus relentlessly on her cleavage.

Statuesque women are exercising and dancing. One woman bounces energetically on a mechanized horse. The camera focuses on the dancing girl's legs.

51.29.06   The head of woman bobbing up and down.
51.34.06   Feet in stirrups.
51.36.06   The head and shoulders move up and down.
51.39.06   A stockinged leg.
51.42.06   The woman is revealed from the waist up.
51.44.10   A javelin is thrown.
51.45.22   A girl dances – cut to a ladies' basketball game.

The game is captured with a hand-held camera. There is no obvious sense of matching but Kaufman does capture the essential speed of the game. A football match is filmed from in much the same way. Svilova enlivens this sequence by cut-ins of a javelin in flight. The sporting activity comes to an end not with a jump-cut but with an actual *jump* (of an athlete) which is cut to:

53.03.14   Motorbikes race around a track.

The bikes are matched (in reverse) to:

53.08.01   A carousel is matched (by similar screen direction) to:
53.12.04   The motorbikes.
53.15.14   [16/20 point] The jump again as a jump-cut to:
53.17.04   The bikes.

Episode 14: Comparisons: kinetic and political

This episode begins with a street organ. The mechanized figure is of a conductor (surely a metaphor for Vertov). The image is inter-cut with customers on the carousel.

53.27.04   Kaufman is following a motorbike on a motorbike.
The jumping figure reappears before:
53.32.15   An aerial shot of finish line in the motorbike race.
53.34.08   The carousel.
53.36.12   The bike race.
A shot of the (Vertov) conductor mannequin cut to a carousel. The woman rider apes camera turning. The bike race continues. Kaufman is filmed following the race. His progress is matched to:
53.43.16   The woman on the carousel (cut away to matched, blurred point of view shots).
53.55.12   Kaufman in bike pursuit.
53.57.24   The carousel.
54.00.12   Kaufman is travelling in the reverse direction, cross cut with the bikes and the carousel.

The sixth and final reel of the film begins with a whip-pan past a poster for a fiction film (*Green Manuel* [Die Grüne Manuela, Germany 1923]) showing at the 'Proletarian Cinema' (Kiev). Vertov bemoans the infiltration of fiction narcotics. He can reassure supporters of the Cine-Eye with an image of the skyline dominated by the cameraman. The split screen shows the cameraman set up in the top half with a wide street in the bottom half. This image is a reminder of the power of the camera and film-making as a pursuit, even an improvement on reality.

Even Soviet reality was still in need of radical improvement in the twilight of the NEP. The final reel of *The Man with the Movie Camera* is the most overtly political (i.e. anti-NEP) section of the film.
54.51.12   A bar sign.
The camera travels through the window of a beer hall. Women sip wine. From a close up of a glass the cameraman emerges. A pile of lobsters scatter and dance for the camera. Vertov is trying to represent intoxication.
55.25.01   [5/6 point] Beer is doled out.
The camera pans unsteadily past a shop selling icons to rest on the icon of the new order. Lenin's image is above the door of a club (named after Ulyanov i.e. Lenin) in Odessa. In the club a board is rapidly prepared for a game of draughts (by using reverse running film) as is a

chess game. A girl in a shooting gallery mows down symbolic enemies beginning with fascism:

56.32.01   [17/20 point] The woman 'shoots' fascism.

This dangerous political enemy is conjoined to a moral danger: the bottle. A crate of beer bottles comes under fire. When the woman runs out of ammunition, the camera wipes out the remaining bottles.

57.11.14   The façade of a wine shop in Odessa.
57.13.17   The cameraman marches out into the street.
57.21.12   The cameraman marches past the camera towards:
57.24.21   The Lenin Club

To underline the political point Vertov lingers on the sign to allow the viewer to notice that the club is named: 'FIRST FIVE-YEAR PLAN.' This is a clear cinematic seal of approval for the new 'new economic policy'. Vertov makes it abundantly clear that the way forward to a New World is the abandonment of the laxities that have crept in under the guise of NEP.

57.33.09   The female proprietor of the wine ship returns to
                  her trade.

Now Vertov and Svilova utilize Kaufman's footage to visualize sound.

57.37.09   A radio speaker.
57.43.18   A bust of Karl Marx.
57.45.20   A close-up of radio controls.
57.47.20   The radio speaker.
57.48.01   Radio valves.

Disembodied hands manipulate the controls. Workers play chess as images of an accordion and an ear are superimposed onto the speaker. A piano is cross-faded to a mouth (Vertov's) singing.

58.21.04   Music is performed by 'playing' everyday objects.
                  This activity is inter-cut with smiling women
                  workers' faces.

From 58.50 these images are shortened in duration until they reach single frame flashes. Images are overlaid into a visual symphony.

Episode 15: 'The cinema'

59.17.01   The diegesis returns to the cinema. The audience is
                  watching the camera come to life on screen.
59.19.03   The tripod enters screen right.

59.25.19	Cut away: a woman in cinema audience (profile).
59.27	The tripod.
59.33	Cut away: a woman (full face).

These people are in *The Man with the Movie Camera* watching *The Man with the Movie Camera*.

59.55.01	[18/20 point] The camera bows to the audience.
60.16.01	The camera box leaves. A woman in the audience smiles.
60.18.03	A spool of wire is spinning.
60.24.01	The wire appears (superimposed) on the cinema screen.
60.30.01	A close up of a reflection on the wire spool.
60.32.01	The audience,
60.35.03	A split screen dancing/piano/teacher.

Svilova engineers a sequence of the audience apparently watching the split-screen images. Vertov had discussed this kind of organization of material in his early writings e.g. 'The Cine-Eyes, A Revolution':

> Example: the filming of a group of dancers ... The spectator at the ballet follows, in confusion ... a series of scattered perceptions, different for each spectator.
>
> We cannot present this to the film viewer...
>
> [*We require*] forceful transfer of the viewer's eyes to the successive details that must be seen.
>
> The camera 'carries' the film viewers' eyes from arms to legs, from legs to eyes and so on, in the most advantageous sequence and organizes the details into an orderly montage study.[30]

60.47.12	An eye level shot of the audience (which contains some heavily made-up 'NEP women') is cut to:
60.57.21	[11/12 point] to fresh faced young dancer 'on screen'.
61.07.17	Kaufman poses with a gun.

The imagery is obvious – and Vertov is making a strong political point. His camera will work as well as a gun in the political struggle ahead.

61.09.22	Aeroplanes.
61.14.01	Kaufman.
61.15.12	Planes on the screen in the cinema.
61.19.19	Kaufman takes aim.

| 61.23.21 | The trams. |
| 61.28.22 | A severely canted shot of switchboard operators. |

This shot could not have been filmed at this angle. It is an example of how the editing process shapes reality.

61.31.07	Trams (in split screen – top image moves towards audience. The lower image moves away).
61.36.01	Split-screen: multiple images of the switchboard.
61.39.02	Trams (top in movement left to right, lower half in movement away).
61.46.07	Split-screen – typing pool.
61.50.01	An audience reaction shot.
61.52.05	The typist superimposed on her keyboard.
61.56.16	Audience reactions.
61.59.13	Multiple superimposition of machinery.
62.06.01	A talking worker (woman) is superimposed over spinning machine.

This worker is presented as an icon of the new Soviet woman. The circular movement of the machinery creates a halo around her head. The axle point is situated in the centre of her forehead.

| 62.12.19 | Kaufman is riding on a motorbike (and turning the camera). |

The cameraman is shown on the screen of the cinema. His motion/position is then *absolutely* matched to:

| 62.18.03 | Kaufman on his bike (full screen) |
| 62.20.07 | Back again but match is reverse direction. |

| 62.26.20 | A crowd: |

This image is *constructed* from a multiply-printed crowd scene. This technique prefigures the digital manipulation of actuality.

62.29.12	(Multiple images of) trams cross right to left.
62.32.07	The train is travelling right to left (full screen) with an absolute match to:
62.33.09	The train on screen.

Vertov and Svilova clearly enjoy this effect of cutting between a full-screen image and one of the shot on a screen (or *vice-versa*). This is more than a very clever piece of editing. The Cine-Eyes are demonstrating the distancing nature of projection even as they themselves project images.

62.38.19	The city crowd (constructed of multiple images).
62.44.20	A woman in the audience: cuts to reaction shots of various audience members.
62.48.03	The Kiev cab driver.
62.50.23	Audience reaction shots (repeated).
62.55.07	A tram turns right as camera sweeps left to:
62.59.19	Audience laughing to (at?):
63.00.13	'NEP woman' disembarks from a tram – cut back to audience.
63.04.01	A push bike.
63.05.12	'NEP woman' in the audience (8 frames).
63.05.21	Walking feet.
63.09.09	A well dressed woman in the audience (8 frames).
63.09.18	A different well dressed woman strides down street.

The mid-point of her progress across screen is at 63.10.12 [19/20 point]. The audience in the cinema is now linked individually and collectively by eye-line matches to various images captured from life: a car, a motorbike with sidecar and the ubiquitous trams and trains. Here Vertov is making connections between his film process and its hoped for audience. He is also asking us (the viewers outside of his diegesis) to be aware of and to question the process we are going through as we watch his film.

Episode 16: 'A new world'

It is important to note and to understand that the New World presented in the final episode of the film is entirely constructed from material we have already seen. The first shot of this episode echoes the first shot of the film.

63.39.08	'The man with the movie camera' is superimposed above the crowd. The camera pans to create a 'camera-line match' to:
63.47.04	A pendulum.
63.50.12	The Bolshoi Theatre implodes (in a split screen effect) to a 90 degree angle.

This image is surely an ideogram: 'Art is dead. Long live the unplayed cinema.'

64.02.21	The pendulum filmed at 12 fps to create an effect of acceleration.

64.06.01	The curtains part in the cinema (animation) to reveal the riders in the Kiev cab (from 'the chase' episode).
64.09.21	A (different) pendulum is also projected at double speed.
64.11.18	The Kiev cab riders (at double speed).
64.16.18	Kaufman is projected onto the screen in the cinema.

After a brief fade to black there is an absolute match to Kaufman on the motorbike (full shot).

This is an interesting order. The process of showing on the screen is shown *before* the full shot. Thus Vertov shows how the image is exhibited before showing how it was shot. For 17 seconds Vertov and Svilova cut backwards and forwards between these two images intercut with (10–12 frame) shots of the cab passengers. There is also a brief cut-in of a street corner (Moscow–the Manège Square in front of the National Hotel) and the bridge seen in the opening 'cameraman' sequence.

64.45.05	A plane flies over.
64.49.17	The beach (projected at double speed),
64.52.01	The Kiev train,
64.55.11	Tverskaia Street is projected at double speed.

From this point all the footage is shown at 24fps but filmed at 18, 16, finally 12 frames per second.

| 65.00.11 | The revolving door, |
| 65.00.21 | A tram stop – in this shot the action is run *backwards*. |

As if to stress that the Cine-Eye can choose the direction of action, Vertov cuts to:

| 65.06.01 | The revolving door. |

This icon of change is followed by a series of three-second shots: a street corner (which seems to have been slowed down) – the door again; Tverskaia Street is displayed in split screen – the door – the street.

The train passes over (on screen), the market, the train passes over (full screen) echoing the order of Kaufman's ride, cars moving past (the end of the funeral from 'life caught unawares' episode), Kaufman on a car, a train, Tverskaia Street.

Twenty four frame shots (Kaufman and Tverskaia Street) are

followed by ten frame shots (film on an editing light box and Svilova) and by four frame shots (Svilova, the train track [the train rushes over left to right], the market). These images are intercut for six seconds.

66.11.01   A tram is displayed with a 'flash' superimposition of Svilova's eyes.

The editor's eyes are giving life and meaning to single or double frame flashes. Moving bodies are flashed in front of a tram. The whole image is tightened by use of a telephoto lens. The blur is interrupted and given meaning by:

66.12.23   A beam of light (from the projector) intercut with shots of trams and Svilova.

Even the editor is 'caught unawares' but then she organizes her own image!

66.17.01   The signal turns back as it is intercut with Svilova's eyes (shots of 2 frames duration). The signal turns back again.

66.25.21   The eye in the lens.

The eye (Vertov's eye) in the lens has become iconographic of 'documentary.' This image is usually seen as a still[31] but it needs to be seen, as it is in the film i.e. *moving*. The 'Cine-Eye' is not the (still) camera eye. It captures moving pictures.

66.26.15   The iris begins to close.

66.28.21   A fade to black and fade up to:

6.30.01   THE END

The pace continues to increase as film passes a light-box and the editor's eye fills the screen. These final moments remind us that this film is as much an editor's *tour de force* as a record of the cameraman's life. This breathtaking flood of images leaves the audience either excited or bemused. We should turn to Vertov to discover the intentional effect of this. For Vertov the cameraman's journey of discovery has revealed and explained 'Life's chaos ...' which 'gradually becomes clear as he observes and shoots.' What is it that is revealed?

Nothing is accidental. everything is explicable and governed by law ... The camera is present at the great battle between two worlds: that of the capitalists, profiteers, factory bosses, and landlords and that of workers, peasants, and colonial slaves.[32]

The dichotomy between capital and labour seems to have landed on the cutting room floor. What is more evident is the last vestiges of 'NEPism' and implicit criticism of various forms of anti-social activity. If the film was to have had an 'international' theme it has been lost in a Soviet-specific analysis.

Vertov has given us perhaps the best description of how this film should strike its audience: 'a 100 per cent film-object, the concentrated essence of "I see" – I cine-see.'[33] He was also keen to make the point that the film was more than a technical miracle. He was very particular to stress the importance of (making) connections:

> The man with the movie camera marches apace with life, to the bank and the club, the pub and the clinic, the Soviet and the housing council, the cooperative and the school, the demonstration and the Party cell meeting. The man with the movie camera manages to go everywhere...
>
> He travels. He switches within a week from automobile to the roof of a train, from train to plane, plane to glider ... and so on.
>
> Life's chaos gradually becomes clear as he observes and shoots. Nothing is accidental. Everything can be explained and is governed by law ... each is engaged in necessary labour.[34]

Vertov turns to the material his brother collected. Again he stresses connections (this time of struggle) and ends with an unambiguous political message:

> All these have their meaning – all are victories, great and small, in the struggle of the new and the old, the struggle of revolution and counter-revolution, the struggle of the cooperative against private capital, of the club against the public house, of athletics against debauchery, dispensary against disease. All this is a position won in the struggle for the Soviet land, the struggle against a lack of faith in socialist construction.

Thus Vertov can explain the 'visual apotheosis' as a political act:

> Life, the film studio and the movie camera at its socialist post.[35]

The film's 'visual apotheosis' is contained in its exceptionally careful structuring. Sequences can be read as short narratives in themselves. Sectioning, and in particular the placing of images at key temporal moments, point to the political content of the film. At particularly significant temporal divisions in the film Vertov brings together calls for action with images of the problems which must be solved. Thus at the quarter point of the film (16.37.01), Kaufman begins his journey into the market.

Perhaps the clearest example of this use of temporal positioning comes at the mid-point of the film [33.15]. The washing and cleansing sequence coming as it does after the juxtaposition of working woman and the beauty parlour creates a message: purge (*chistit'*). This call for cleansing has already been made at an early key sectional moment in the film. At the 1/6 point (11.05.01) Vertov places a close-up of the hosing down of street lamps.

As the film reaches its final (1/12) section an eye level shot of the cinema audience shows it to contain some heavily made-up 'NEP women'. At the 11/12 point (60.57.22) there is a cut from an NEP woman in audience to a fresh faced young dancer 'on screen'. This move from the old to the new echoes the 1/12 point of the film (5.34.01) which features the film's first shot of the Bolshoi Theatre. This most potent icon of the old ways (of 'Art' and social organization) will be exploded at the end of the film.

Throughout the film Vertov placed 'the movie camera at its socialist post'. The themes that Vertov explores and highlights in his carefully constructed diegesis centre on what constitutes a healthy society. He also focuses unflinchingly on the methods required to achieve his vision of that healthy society. These themes remain significant particularly to continued attempts to understand the historical phenomenon that was the Soviet Union. Vertov's desire (and attempt) to decode reality remains significant to anyone interested in documentary practice. Further consideration of the film's continuing significance constitutes the final chapter of this book.

Notes

1   O. Blakeston 'Three Russian Films', *Close Up* vol. V, no. 2 (August 1929), p. 144.
2   'The Cine-Eyes: A Revolution', *Lef* 3, 1923, *SD* p. 56, *KE* p. 18, *FF* p. 93.
3   V. Petrić, *Constructivism in Film. The Man with the Movie Camera: A Cinematic Analysis*, Cambridge, 1987, pp. 72–78.

4   From Tsivian's commentary to the BFI video.

5   Kaufman interviewed in *October* no. 3, Winter 1979.

6   *SD* pp. 277–279, *KE* pp. 283–9.

7   *SD* p. 72, *KE* p. 41–2.

8   The Russian word *opyt* can also be translated as 'experience'.

9   *peredacha* could be translated as 'communication' or 'broadcast.'

10   'The Man with the Movie Camera' *SD* p. 277, *KE* p. 283.

11   ibid.

12   ibid.

13   In the commentary to BFI video.

14   see chapter 2, p. 25.

15   *SD* p. 280, *KE* pp. 286–7.

16   This film was directed by Fred Sauer. It is also known as *The Girl Downstairs*.

17   This technical trick has some contemporary resonance. The trailers for Hollywood 'blockbusters' e.g. *Twister* (1996) and *Armageddon* (1998) use this effect to build audience excitement and expectation.

18   Petrić, pp. 164–76.

19   Mikhail Kaufman quoted in *October*, no. 3 1979.

20   See chapter 2, p. 16.

21   S. Feldman 'The Harmony of Man and Machine' – a quotation from the original manuscript supplied by the author. This article has since been published in B. Grant and J. Sloniowski *Documenting the Documentary*, Detroit MI., 1999)

22   L. Schapiro *The Communist Party of the Soviet Union*, London, 1970, p. 324.

23   see next chapter p. 101.

24   V. Shklovskii, 'Sergei Eisenstein and 'Non-played' Film', *FF* p. 161.

25   *SD* p. 45, *KE* p. 6, a somewhat different translation appears in *FF* p. 69.

26   *SD* p. 282, *KE* p. 289.

27   'We the shoemakers of cinematography say to you, the shoe-shiners, that we do not recognize your seniority.' 'On the Significance of Unplayed Cinema', *SD* p. 67, *KE* p. 37.

28   Feldman 'The Harmony of Man and Machine'.

29   Tsivian is right to draw parallels between Vertov's aesthetic and the work of Walt Whitman, particularly 'I Sing the Body Electric'.

30   *SD* p. 54, *KE* p. 16, *FF* pp. 92–3.

31   e.g. the front cover of Brian Winston's *Claiming the Real*, London, 1995.

32   'The Man with the Movie Camera (A Visual Symphony)' *SD* p. 282, *KE* pp. 288–9.

33   *SD* p. 115, *KE* p. 90.

34   *SD* p. 281, *KE* pp. 289.

35   ibid.

4. Signification and Significance

'A "higher mathematics" of facts'

Dziga Vertov 1928[1]

It is easy to be dazzled by *The Man with the Movie Camera*. Even a basic knowledge of cinematography and a cursory acquaintance with the history of cinema would lead a viewer to a state of awe after a single viewing. However, to justify continued study of the film it is important to ask: is it more than a 'box of tricks' which deserves a footnote in the history of cinema? What does the film mean – what does all this bravura film-making signify? What *is* its lasting significance?

The second chapter of this book has attempted to show that the film is worthy of attention due to its historical significance. Chapter 3 has – I believe – made a case for *The Man with the Movie Camera* as a significant piece of film-making. This final chapter will argue for the film's continuing significance in a number of areas. Reference will be made to Vertov's role in Modernism and his position in Soviet culture. By a logical extension this approach will position Vertov within the context of developments in Soviet politics after the film's release. Finally I will explain the film's position as a key text in the history and study of film.

Vertov and (Soviet) Modernism

As an avowedly political film-maker it is practically impossible to remove Vertov, his work practice or even any of his work from the political milieu. However, there are certain aesthetic, technical and thematic issues which are *sui generis* to Vertov and his position as a Modernist which cannot be ignored.

Feldman argues that 'Vertov's 1929 trip abroad went far in establishing him as an international film personality.'[2] In the West, he became, and remained, the personification of the Soviet 'modern'. Others died like Mayakovsky, ossified – like Gorky, or became a symbol of resistance to, rather than justification for, Soviet power. Vertov remained, whether he liked it or not, always the politically committed experimenter, the Constructivist famed for his ability to celebrate the power of Soviet Communism in the machine and the city. To a large extent it was *The Man with the Movie Camera* (and *Enthusiasm*) which created and sealed this image.

European Modernism was an urban phenomenon. Vertov's film can of course be seen as a study of *the* – not *a* – city. However, his celebration of the urban goes beyond that of his contemporaries. When touring Europe he bridled against the German critics when they suggested that his work was a more 'fanatical extension of the theory and practice of Ruttmann'[3] Vertov suggested – rather peevishly – that Ruttmann copied him rather than the reverse.

It is also worth noting that Ruttmann was portraying a single city. Vertov was *constructing* a representation of a new one from images of three old ones (Moscow, Kiev and Odessa). In addition, as Kracauer noted of Ruttmann, 'he actually tends to avoid any critical comment on the reality with which he is faced.'[4] Vertov plunges in, praising the 'politically correct', damning the incorrect, and making a bold attempt to change the reality he observes.

The European cinema tradition of representing the city usually contains at least a note of caution. This can be seen in classics like Lang's *Metropolis* (1926), innumerable French films on the moral perils of city life and British thrillers of the 1920s, including Hitchcock's early work culminating with *Blackmail* (1929). Documentary shorts and features of the 1920s dwell pruriently on crime and unhealthy conditions. For Vertov the city is not a dystopia, although it does have a seedy underside. The negative aspects of city life are vestiges of capitalism and can be swept away. His film suggests that this process can be achieved by increased reliance on technology. Indeed at times the film seems to suggest that the technology can be set in motion and allowed to complete the task itself.

Unlike the films produced in the USA, see for example Vidor's *The Crowd* [1929], Chaplin's *City Lights* [1931] or *Modern Times* [1936], *The Man with the Movie Camera* is a celebration rather than a condemnation. Vertov appreciates the possibilities and potentials of urban development. At the end of *Modern Times* the Tramp and the girl walk *away* from the city. In *The Man with the Movie Camera* Mikhail Kaufman's camera rushes through and over the city relishing the speed of movement and the variety of material. The cameraman, after his 'holiday', returns to the city with a joyous embrace.

Clearly the subject of the film is also a matter of the process as well as of the urban material. I have previously suggested that it is not too strong to suggest that by the time of *The Man with the Movie Camera* Vertov, with a philosophical position close to the Futurists, had developed a visual style which is not so much *Constructivist* as *productionist*.[5] In this approach the project of production is not only celebrated on screen but also in *the way it is presented* on screen – including the conscious presentation of the film production itself.[6] The film is a purely visual contribution to specifically Soviet Modernism. In this way Vertov is at least as important a theorist as Alexei Gan[7] and goes further in showing how his way of seeing the world can be translated into cinematic reality.

Even in 1929, Vertov was struggling to explain or justify himself. He was already being ghettoized into the Modernist deadend of 'difficult' or for 'specialists' only. This was made clear in the 'Letter from Berlin':

> The fact that the Berlin press is not aware of the Cine-Eyes' chronological developments and its decade of attack on the stronghold of played film can only be explained by incorrect, false information (or a complete lack of information) on this issue...

Even his self-defence contains an admittance of failure to reach a wide audience:

> The Cine-Eye workers have not the least doubt that their work, both theoretical and practical, though inadequately distributed, is perfectly familiar to the majority of professionals.[8]

Plus ça change for Vertov. The situation was even worse at home.

Vertov and The Soviet Union

The Soviet response to *The Man with the Movie Camera* was cool. The film industry simply rejected the film as unsuitable for domestic audiences. The problem for Vertov was that by 1929 Soviet cinema was expected to have moved on from experimentation to mature political responsibility. The continuing negative reaction to each of Vertov's subsequent films can be seen as evidence of the nature of the Stalinist hegemony which was already developing in the late 1920s.

Khersonsky wrote in *Kino* of 'narrow formalism and technical fetishism: 'Vertov remains the "artist child" of the "artistic infancy" of Soviet cinema.'[9] Lenobl attacked the film for 'technological fetishism'[10] (and conflated Vertov's approach with the sorts of 'experts' who came under increasing suspicion after the Shakhty trial).

In September 1929 RAPP (the Russian Association of Proletarian Writers) in a 'Resolution on Cinema' went so far as to state:

> The concept of revolutionary cinema has sometimes been identified with the concept of 'left' cinema and this has given the Formalists the chance to camouflage themselves as 'revolutionaries' and declare 'revolutionary' any formal experiments, even this devoid of social content (Dziga Vertov's *The Man with the Movie Camera*).[11]

Other film-makers were far from sympathetic. Vertov had consistently failed to be fair to them. Shub remained quiet, but that in itself should be read as implicit criticism from an ally. Eisenstein took the opportunity to disparage Vertov's latest work in a discussion of the use of slow motion: 'Even more frequently it is used simply for formal trifles and pointless mischief with the camera, as in *The Man with the Movie Camera*.'[12]

Mikhail Kaufman's response to his brother's film is interesting even though it was (at the time and long afterwards) entirely muddled. Vertov and Svilova edited the film in a way which left Kaufman confused and upset.[13] He never grasped that in *The Man with The Movie Camera* the (cine) eyes are Vertov's or Svilova's. Kaufman *is* the 'Man with the Movie Camera,' i.e. the *star* of the film not its *auteur*. After *The Man with the Movie Camera* Kaufman made a most professional (if rather dull) movie entitled *Springtime* [Vesnoi, 1929] which he saw as the second half of *The Man with the Movie Camera*. Vertov refused to work on it. The brothers did not work together again. Vertov's 'Council of Three' was reduced to two.

The contemporary Soviet audience response to *The Man with the Movie Camera* remains a mystery. Later critics such as Vlada Petrić

– wishing to claim Vertov for the esoteric ends of the avant garde –
have positively avoided any reference to the audience for the film.
Contemporary information must, like all Soviet materials, be taken
with a large pinch of salt. Denise Youngblood refers to an article by
N. Kaufman, no relation but a long-term advocate of Vertov's work,
who claimed that any lack of audience response was due to limited
runs and rental 'politics'.[14] She also notes that an article in *Sovetskii
Ekran* (no. 17, 1929) claimed *The Man with the Movie Camera* was a
financial success. This claim seems as unlikely as any other made in
the increasingly unreliable world of the Soviet cinema press.

Massive changes were instituted in the cinema industry during and
after the making of *The Man with the Movie Camera* which would leave
its 'author-supervisor' increasingly isolated. These changes continued
and accelerated the course set out with the decrees and conferences of
1928 and 1929. Serious attempts to change fundamentally the
personnel of the industry began with the change (and associated purge)
from Sov- (i.e. Soviet) to Soiuz- (i.e Union) kino as the state cinema
organization. Increased centralization and increased control of cadres
was a direct, long-term result of the Central Committee directive. Boris
Shumiatsky was installed as head of the new cinema agency.[15]

The change in approach in the press had already been signalled by
the name change from *Sovetskii ekran* [Soviet Screen] to *Kino i zhizn'*
[Cinema and Life] – the 'mass illustrated magazine for cinematography' – in November 1929. The change of title is significant. The use
of the word 'life' (*zhizn'*) signals a more practical approach to cinema
where the cinema is a tool rather than the absolute centre of interest.
The new editor – Yakov Rudnoi – addressed his readers thus:

> Our new magazine appears at a moment of intensified class struggle
> in the country of the grandiose victory of socialist construction ...
> (the struggle) has to take place on an ideological front, on the front
> of art, for honesty in cinematography, where frequently under the
> flag of all sorts of genres, artistic schools and directions have wrig-
> gled through petit-bourgeois tendencies, which it is necessary to
> rebuff decisively.[16]

The editor goes on to join battle with 'formalism, aestheticism and the
other vices of bourgeois "art for art"' and promises to 'struggle to fulfil
the decisions of the party in the area of cinema'. The article ends:

'[*Kino i zhizn*] will be fighting ... for a form of cinema art accessible to the millions' and a quote from Lenin: '[Art] must be intelligible to the masses and loved by them.' The film which came in for most praise in the early months of 1930 was Viktor Turin's *Turksib*.[17]

Vertov was already planning his first sound film *Enthusiasm* in the autumn of 1929.[18] His team filmed during the following spring and summer. The finished picture was previewed in November 1930 and released in April 1931.

To quote Feldman:

As was the case with *Man with the Movie Camera*, Vertov had, with *Enthusiasm*, created a work that reflected the aesthetic of the Soviet avant-garde. By 1931, however, that avant-garde was well on the way to being entirely decimated. Mayakovsky's suicide, an event which marked the symbolic end of the movement, had taken place the year before.[19] Other Soviet artists of a 'leftist' bent had either gone abroad or suffered at home. It may well have seemed dangerously ironic to Ukrainfilm [the renamed VUFKU] executives to see the celebration of the completion of the Five Year Plan – an event which consolidated Stalin's power – depicted in a style the Soviet leader so openly deplored.[20]

As had been the case with *The Man with the Movie Camera*, having supplied Soviet authorities with an unusable movie Vertov and his film were 'exported'. On his 1931 tour Vertov visited several European cities including London, where he famously fought the projectionist at the Film Society and received fulsome praise (for the film not the fight) from Chaplin.[21]

Shortly after the release of *Enthusiasm* a debate emerged in the cinema press about 'documentalism'.[22] The debate was launched in the pages of the newly retitled (with clear class-struggle purpose) *Proletarskoe kino* [Proletarian Cinema].[23] Early numbers of the magazine made it clear that its view of cinema would be strictly functionalist. In May 1931 an article by Ivan Borisov entitled 'The Documentalists and Sound Cinema' appeared. It is about more than that. The article begins with a section of the *Izvestiia* review of *Symphony of the Donbas* written by Radek: 'no advancement ... lack of dynamics ... it is a stride backwards in Soviet cinema.' Borisov attacks the: 'Narrow-mindedness which proclaims itself above all in the fetishism of fact and dogma of the spontaneous.'[24] The article concentrates its real ire on Vertov's 'leftist negative art'.

Proletarskoe kino continued its 'self-critical' discussion of the documentary question in edition no. 5, 1932. The editorial continued to set up the debate between Erofeyev, Vertov and Lebedev.[25] Vertov attacked Lebedev in edition no. 5 in the following disgraceful (and dangerous) vein:

> At that time [1925] the viewpoint of N. Lebedev on cinema concurred not with the views of Lenin on cinema, but with the point of view of Trotsky ... his point of view, the point of view of Lebedev-Trotsky [tochka zrenii Lebedeva-Trotskogo] set itself against 'the Lenin Proportion'.[26]

Later in this edition Erofeyev attacked Lebedev as following: 'the Trotskyite conception of cinematography'.

Observing film-makers constructing their own 'show-trials' is an unedifying sight. Involvement did Vertov no good. He had expressed 'Trotskyite' – i.e. anti NEP – views in the mid-1920s. These 'mistakes', as they were viewed with hindsight, could only draw more suspicion on him and his work. Vertov's ostentatiously stated position of *not* using a scenario was by definition 'anti-planning' at a time when 'The Plan' was all. Vertov's whole career up to this point could be seen as subversive to the new Party orthodoxy. This, along with the perfectly reasonable view that his work was difficult, would be a major reason his problems – not least a lack of resources – continued into the 1930s and beyond.

A defining factor in Vertov's predicament was the antipathy of the leadership of the industry, personified by Boris Shumiatsky. As Richard Taylor put it:

> He saw it as his job to turn Soviet cinema into what he called a 'cinema of the millions'... above all with films that were, in the catchphrase of the critiques of the later 1920s, 'intelligible to the millions'.[27]

The 'cinema question' was a functional question. The central issue was to get the (political) message across. The key was plot not montage:

A plotless form for a work of art is powerless to express an idea of any significance ... among our masters you will find people who say: 'I am working on a plot-less, story-less level.'
People who maintain that position are profoundly deluded.[28]

In the spring of 1933 Vertov began work on a film 'About Lenin' (a project he had been trying to sell to Ukrainfilm since the summer of 1932). The film – which became *Three Songs about Lenin* – was finally commissioned by the Mezhrabpom studio in Moscow. Vertov struggled with a paucity of archive film and the hostility of bureaucracy. In addition he found working in Central Asia tiresome.

The film should have been premiered on 24 January 1934 (the tenth anniversary of Lenin's death). In fact it did not open until November. As Feldman notes, the release of *Three Songs about Lenin* was overshadowed by the arrival of the Vasilievs' *Chapayev.* Here at last was the new Soviet cinema: a simple story simply told with an obvious political moral clearly explained.[29] Vertov would receive the Order of the Red Star in 1935 – but he and his work were to be ignored.

Vertov was a defeated man. His later work, including the chilling Stalinist hagiography *Lullaby* [Kolybelnaia, 1937] is well made but lacks the earlier visual panache. Unable to make full-length films after *Sergo Ordzhonikidze* in 1937, he continued editing the central newsreel *News of the Day* [Novosti dnia] until he died on 12 February 1954.

The Soviet revival of Vertov's reputation came as part of the flowering of all things which could be grasped as 'anti-Stalinist' in the early 1960s. That there was any reputation to revive was due almost entirely to Svilova's refusal to let her late husband's memory fade or to allow his archive to be dispersed. Thus Sergei Drobashenko was able to publish Vertov's articles, diaries and projects in 1966 as a late example of 'the Thaw'. Even the context of this revival tended to push Vertov into the realms of avant-garde originator rather than the political film-maker. This would not be so much the case, at least initially, in the revival in the West. Before reaching that point it is interesting to see how Western critics contemporary to Vertov viewed his masterpiece.

Vertov and the Critics

The Man with the Movie Camera would remain a buried masterpiece if it had simply been one of many, admittedly less brilliant, pieces of film-making crumbling in the archives. Its significance goes beyond the status of being an early victim of the Stalinist repression in the arts.

Controversies about the film and the, rarely less than extreme, reaction not to say arguments of critics, historians and theorists are evidence of a fascination about the film. They show its continuing significance in the sense that it continues to prove itself worthy of attention.

The critical responses of Vertov's contemporaries were in part split by geographical location. I have already noted above that the Soviet film industry contained elements within it that had good reason to dislike Vertov and his work. They found *The Man with the Movie Camera* as easy to attack as any of his films. In Germany Vertov received polite if bemused interest[30] mixed with genuine praise, which Vertov later used in self-publicity campaigns.

Amongst the audience of the Paris showing/lecture in 1929 was Georges Rouquier, who began film-making in 1929 and made his masterpiece of 'life caught unawares' with *Farrebique* in 1946.[31]

The British cinema establishment showed their usual suspicion of anything that moved away from 'realism'. Grierson dismissed Vertov's work, including *The Man with the Movie Camera*, in a 1929 review of the film: 'Vertov has pushed the argument to a point at which it becomes ridiculous.'[32] Grierson was no more 'enthusiastic' about *Symphony of the Donbas*:

> It is all dazzle – dazzle and bits and pieces, whoopee for this, whoopee for that! – like any masterwork of the close-up school. But body of thought or body of construction, it has none.[33]

Paul Rotha reminisced later that: 'Vertov was regarded really as rather a joke you know. All this cutting, and one camera photographing another camera – it was all trickery, and we didn't take it seriously.'[34]

In the English-speaking world at least the Griersonian tradition retained its hegemony. Seth Feldman has written with great perception on the intrinsic differences between the Grierson (or indeed Robert Flaherty) approach and Vertov's methodology, particularly in his attempt to move away from 'individual' actors and the lack of exoticism in his anthropological work.[35] Also in contrast to Grierson and co. Vertov is unashamedly an active part of the world he is investigating, criticizing and for which he is prescribing solutions to its problems. This is a position that Flaherty and particularly Grierson would have found abhorrent.

Vertov did have his influence in the United States. Leyda himself remembers *The Man with the Movie Camera* as the first Soviet film he ever saw, in New York in 1930: 'a full to bursting film, recognized abroad for what it really is, an avant-garde film.'[36] He reeled from the cinema unable to watch the film (ever) again but convinced he must study in Moscow.

Samuel Brody's exposure to Vertov's work led to the formation of the Worker's Film and Photo League in 1931. Brody had translated Vertov's Paris lecture in 1929 into English[37] and has the honour of at least attempting to underline Vertov's role as a *political* film-maker.

The emergence of a politically motivated documentary movement in Europe in the 1960s led to a more recent reassessment and indeed a rise in Vertov's perceived value as a film-maker.

Jean Rouch, a social scientist interested in technology, turned to ethnographic film-making in the 1950s. His *cinéma vérité* work, e.g. *Story of a Summer* [Chronique d'un été, 1961] on 'the strange tribe that lives in Paris', could be described as 'life caught unawares'. Rouch certainly claimed kinship: 'I'm one of the people responsible for this phrase [cinéma vérité] and it's really a homage to Vertov.'[38] The other French film-maker who could claim to be continuing the Vertov tradition was Chris Marker, but he always preferred to stress the influence of Medvedkin.[39]

Vertov was rediscovered in the West due in no small part to the heroic efforts of Georges Sadoul. It was he who chose to translate *Kinopravda* as '*cinéma vérité*', as he did in his article: 'Actualité de Dziga Vertov' in the influential *Cahiers du Cinema*.[40] Seth Feldman extends the *Cahiers* link to make a claim for Vertov being an influence on the *nouvelle vague* 'who were taking cameras into the streets and finding their stories in the lives of ordinary people'.[41]

In the 1960s 'counter cinema' movement no less a key figure than Jean-Luc Godard was attracted to an, admittedly mythologized, image of Vertov which mixed formalism and communism.[42] Godard, with Jean-Pierre Gorin, formed 'The Dziga Vertov Group'. When Vertov's articles and notebooks were translated into French in 1972, Godard welcomed the volume as a 'little red book'.

In the USA, Peter Kubelka restored *Enthusiasm* at Anthology Film Archives and showed Vertov alongside the American avant-garde (e.g.

Maya Deren). Vertov's linkage with American art cinema led to his discovery by Annette Michelson, who championed him as 'cinema's Trotsky'[43] and introduced *Kino Eye*, Kevin O'Brien's (American) English translation of Vertov's articles, diaries and projects published in 1984.

Michelson clearly positions *The Man with the Movie Camera* as 'the key film-text for the generation of film-makers who called into question the grounds and claims of cinematic representation through the political uprisings of 1968.'[44]

In her introduction to *Kino Eye* Michelson attempts to position Vertov within an aesthetic *and* a political context. She (with absolute justification) chooses to link Vertov with the visual arts as 'the formulation of a semantics of socialist construction'.[45] Michelson seeks to associate Vertov closely with Malevich and particularly Tatlin. The linking of Vertov and Tatlin is entirely justifiable. It positions Vertov as a political artist and as Constructivist. It is true that Vertov's work grew out of Constructivism. However I have already argued that by the time of *The Man with the Movie Camera* Vertov had moved on to a 'productionist' view.

One eminent, and eloquent, voice which has been raised in praise of Vertov has chosen to take a more purely formalist view. It would be absurd to write a book about *The Man with the Movie Camera* without paying due deference to Vlada Petrić's work. *Constructivism in Film* is a magnificent achievement. However I have a number of major difficulties with the book. I am at variance with an attempt to make Vertov the preserve of 'art', i.e. unpopular, cinema.

Petrić does not help in dispelling Vertov's 'difficult' reputation. I agree with him (and Noel Burch) that the film 'demands that the spectator take an active role as decipherer of its images'. It is true that:

This film is not made to be viewed once. It is impossible for anyone to assimilate this work in a single viewing ... that it is impossible to fully decipher the film's discourse until one has a complete topographical grasp of the film as a whole, in other words after several viewings.[46]

However, I will not concur with Petrić that it is:

necessary not only to see this film several times, but to examine each sequence and even individual shots on an analyst projector or editing table.[47]

My problems with Petrić's approach are essentially in three areas. Firstly I find his 'Social and Political Commentary' (pp. 107–9) rather bland: sweating workers *are* juxtaposed with NEP-women, but as part of a whole network of associations. The winos in the park are juxtaposed with a giant bottle (but it is *water*). Secondly I cavil against the somewhat ornate use of language which often obscures clear analysis of cinematic technique. Finally, and again stressing how stimulating Petrić's work is, I must warn potential readers that his analysis of formal structure does seems to overwrite the difficulties of analysis.

Whilst writing this book I have taken the opportunity of corresponding with the West's leading Vertovian: Seth Feldman. He has been able to aid me with details and never less than stimulating opinions. It is a tribute to the power of Vertov's vision that Seth has recently returned to analysis of *The Man with the Movie Camera* with: 'Peace Between Man and Machine'[48] in which he positions Vertov as a radical film-maker in practice and politics:

> He was ever the good Futurist-Constructivist-Bolshevik, writing the history of the Revolution not on paper but with a technological manifestation of the future it promised.
>
> The film would be a remembrance of optimism past. It is because he believed that, he wished his film to be as polished an argument as he could make it.[49]

Feldman is particularly subtle in his exploration of Vertov's greatest work as an attempt to bridge the gap between 'Life Caught Unawares and the Cinema Eye'. He positions the bridge absolutely (and absolutely correctly) in the editing:

> For while the images we see are invariably the product of the ubiquitous camera, their arrangement points to visions possible only in cinema ... Editing is thus again a way of splicing the mechanical to the human, of making 'peace between man and machine'. In *The Man with the Movie Camera*'s climactic sequence, it is the editing between the audience watching the film and the images on the screen which links us, as viewers, with the viewers within the film.

Politically (including the politics of Vertov's disputes with ᴜᴇ Soviet cinema industry), the point of the montage is to tell us that this is our cinema too.[50]

I must concur with Feldman when he states that – now we are past Vertov's and cinema's centenary: 'Citing Vertov's work as archetypal of the modernist avant-garde is an undertaking which seems to have run its course ...' Feldman prefers to position Vertov as an innovator working at the absolute cutting edge of film technique and technology. This leads to the possibility of a contemporary resonance:

the prototype of the net surfer downloading the bits and pieces of fragmented information. Vertov the film-maker – and advocate of mass film-making – could well be thought of as a pioneer in the building of a system in which millions of people reconstruct those fragments.[51]

The Man with the Movie Camera as the first 'webcast'? This may be a forced parallel, but Denis Kaufman – aka the 'spinning gypsy' – would have been proud of the association.

Conclusion: Vertov and the Aesthetics of the Political

My admiration for *The Man with the Movie Camera* goes beyond even Feldman's recognition of Vertov as the consummate innovator and visionary. For me the fascination of the film lies in the ability to combine cinematic virtuosity with a deeply held desire to change the world. The fact that, a decade after the passing of the Soviet Union, Vertov's political aims seem at least curious, certainly naïve and finally sinister does not diminish the fascination of the film.

Vertov produced a film that was a product of personal, artistic and cinematic crisis made against a backdrop of domestic and international political turmoil and the beginnings of a social and economic maelstrom. As a militant in film-making and political terms he could not fail to produce a masterpiece.

The Man with the Movie Camera is constructed with a mathematical precision. Beyond structural considerations, the choice and juxtaposition of images is never less than intriguing. Even while being intrigued the viewer should be aware of the Cine-Eye's purpose. Vertov uses and reuses images to give them iconic value. The activities of ordinary people, many of them quite ordinary in themselves, become symbolic of a new order.

Throughout the film Vertov placed 'the movie camera at its socialist post'. The subject matter of *The Man with the Movie Camera* is not only what constitutes the correct path for cinema but also (and inextricably) what constitutes the right path for society. It is all too easy to be carried away by the virtuoso technique of this most technically brilliant of films. However, the viewer should never forget that this film is a product of that period of, possibly manufactured but nonetheless real, crisis of 1926–9. That crisis engendered a complete overhaul of a state that covered 'One-sixth of the world' in a spirit of 'There are no fortresses that Bolsheviks cannot storm.' As such the film is an absolutely essential document in the understanding of the forces which contributed to the building of the Soviet Union which emerged from the cultural, economic and political revolution of the late 1920s and early 1930s.

The Man with the Movie Camera exemplifies the belief that all things were possible in economic and social transformation. Vertov's manifesto (in print at the beginning of the film and in the visual diegesis) constitutes an end to compromise. For Vertov film-makers to that point had only interpreted the world in various ways; the point however was to change it.

The ability to combine a richly textured political and aesthetic thesis lies at the centre of the film's continuing appeal to audiences and analysts alike. When such thought-provoking subject matter is combined with breathtaking visual elan the result is a masterpiece of world cinema. *The Man with the Movie Camera* is an example of all that cinema can (and let us not forget *does* on occasion) achieve. The film's complexity and intensity made it and still make it a thrilling experience. That we can still be thrilled is a tribute to the power of the moving image and to *The Man with the Movie Camera*.

Notes

1 'The Man with the Movie Camera' *SD* p. 107, *KE* p. 84.
2 S. Feldman, *Dziga Vertov* p. 13.
3 'Letter from Berlin', 8 July 1929, *SD* p. 120, *KE* p. 101.
4 S. Kracauer *From Caligari to Hitler*, London, 1976, p. 187.
5 G. Roberts *Forward Soviet!*, London, 1998, p. 90.

6   As Eric Barnouw puts it in *Documentary*, Oxford, 1983, p. 63 'The film incessantly reminds us that it is a film.'

7   Gan's place in the pantheon of Modernism is reliant on his book *Constructivism* (1922) and editorship of *Kino-Fot* (1922–3). Having produced at least one great film-*maker* in Vertov, the Constructivists outdid their predecessors the Italian Futurists who – at best – produced one significant film: Ginna's *Vita Futurista* [Futurist Life, 1916].

8   'Letter from Berlin', 8 July 1929, *SD* p. 120, *KE* p. 101.

9   *Kino* 7, 1929, p. 4.

10   *Kino* 17, 1929, p. 1.

11   *FF* p. 278.

12   S. M. Eisenstein, 'Beyond the shot' [Za kadrom] – a postscript to N. Kaufman, *Iaponskoe kino* [Japanese Cinema] (Moscow, 1929), translation from Richard Taylor (ed.), *Selected Works, vol. I*, London, 1988, p. 149. This comment should be seen as part of a long-running, indeed personal disagreement between the two masters which goes back to Vertov's attacks on Eisenstein's usurpation of the Cine-Eye method.

13   See previous chapter, p. 44.

14   N. Kaufman, 'Kinoki', *Sovetskii ekran* no. 4, 1929, p. 4, cited in D. Youngblood, *Soviet Cinema* p. 208.

15   An assessment of the crucial role played by Shumiatsky in the history of Soviet cinema can be found in R. Taylor 'Boris Shumyatsky and the Soviet Cinema in the 1930s: Ideology as Entertainment', *Historical Journal of Film, Radio and Television*, vol. 6, no. 1, 1986, reprinted as 'Ideology as Entertainment, Boris Shumiatskii and Soviet Cinema in the 1930s', in R. Taylor and I. Christie (eds), *Inside the Film Factory: New Approaches to Russian and Soviet Film*, London and New York, 1990, pp. 193–216.

16   'K nashim chitateliam', *Kino i zhizn'*, no. 1, 1929.

17   See 'RAPP Resolution on Cinema', *FF* p. 277, I. Sokolov 'The Legend of "Left" Cinema', *FF* p. 288.

18   Feldman, p. 13.

19   See Vertov's increasing identification with Mayakovskii: *SD* pp. 154–9 and 172–94, *KE* pp. 172–86 and 265–6.

20   Feldman, p. 14.

21   T. Dickinson and C. De la Roche, *Soviet Cinema*, London, 1948, p. 3.

22   A much fuller consideration of this debate is contained in my *Forward Soviet!*, pp. 92–108.

23   Launched with the aim 'once and for all of overcoming the experience of class hostility to us from bourgeois cinematography.': 'Chto znachit proletarskoe kino?', *Proletarskoe kino*, no. 1, 1931.

24   I. Borisov, 'Dokumentalisty v zvukovom kino', *Proletarskoe kino*, vol. 5, no, 5, 1931, p. 12.

25   They were aided in this by a long-standing animosity between Vertov and Lebedev originating in Lebedev's accusations of plagiarism in Vertov's *One Sixth of the World*.

26 'Polnaia kapituliatsiia Nikolaia Lebedeva', *Proletarskoe kino*, no. 5, 1932, p. 12.
27 R. Taylor, 'Popular Culture in Soviet Cinema', in A. Lawton (ed.), *The Red Screen*, London, 1992, p. 60.
28 Shumiatskii, B., 'Tvorcheskie zadachi templana', *Sovetskii kino*, no. 12, 1933, p. 6, cited in Taylor 'Popular Culture', pp. 60–1.
29 As recommended by no less than a *Pravda* editorial of 21 November 1934: 'The Whole Country is Watching *Chapayev.*' *FF* pp. 334–5.
30 Vertov's 'Letter from Berlin', ibid.
31 Whilst there are clearly elements of Vertovian 'life caught unawares' in Rouquier's work, it should be noted that Barnouw in *Documentary*, p. 190, counter-claims that he worked 'under the influence of Flaherty'.
32 J. Grierson, *Grierson on the Movies*, London, 1981, Forsyth Hardy (ed.), p. 68.
33 Grierson, p. 128.
34 B. Winston, *Claiming the Real*, p. 166.
35 Feldman, pp. 32–3.
36 Leyda, *Kino*, pp. 251–2.
37 *Kinofront*, vol. 1 no. 2, Jan 1935, p. 5 (NB the choice of a 'Sovietized' name for the paper and indeed the homage to the Soviet periodical of that name).
38 G. Roy Levin, *Documentary Explorations*, New York, 1971, p. 131.
39 See Marker's films *The Train Rolled On* and *The Last Bolshevik*.
40 G. Sadoul, 'Actualité de Dziga Vertov', *Cahiers du cinéma*, June 1963, pp. 23–31.
41 S. Feldman, 'Peace between Man and Machine' – original manuscript as supplied to me by the author.
42 Vertov would have refused the formalist label and was never a member of the Communist Party.
43 *KE* p. lxi.
44 *KE* p. xxvii.
45 *KE* p. xxxv.
46 Petrić, *Constructivism in Film*, p. 76.
47 ibid. p. 78.
48 B. Grant and J. Sloniowski (eds.), *Documenting the Documentary*, Detroit, 1998.
49 S. Feldman, 'Peace between Man and Machine'.
50 ibid.
51 ibid.

Further Reading

The Man with the Movie Camera and Dziga Vertov

M. Armour, 'The Machine Art of Dziga Vertov and Busby Berkeley', *Images*, no. 5 (UCLA) 1998.

S. Crofts, and O. Rose, 'An Essay towards *Man with the Movie Camera*', *Screen*, vol. 18, no. 1, 1977, pp. 9–57.

S. Drobashenko, (ed.), *Stat'i, dnevniki, zamysli*, Moscow, 1966, translated as: K. O'Brien, (trans) *Kino-Eye: the Writings of Dziga Vertov*, London, 1984, with an introduction by Annette Michelson.

S. Feldman, *Dziga Vertov: A Guide to References and Resources*, Boston, 1979.

—— *Evolution and Style in the Early Works of Dziga Vertov*, New York, 1975.

—— 'Peace, between Man and Machine: Dziga Vertov's The Man with the Movie Camera', in B. Grant and J. Slioniowski (eds), *Documenting the Documentary*, Detroit, 1999.

V. Petrić, *Constructivism in Film. The Man with the Movie Camera. A Cinematic Analysis*, Cambridge, 1979.

Y. Tsivian, 'Dziga Vertov's Frozen Music: Cue Sheets and a Music Scenario for *The Man with the Movie Camera*', *Griffithiana*, vol. 54, October 1995, pp. 92–121.

Russian and Soviet Film

T. Dickinson, and C. De la Roche, *Soviet Cinema*, London, 1948.

S. M. Eisenstein, Richard Taylor (ed.), *Selected Works Vol I*, London, 1988.

P. Kenez, *Cinema and Soviet Society*, 2nd edn, London, 2000.

A. Lawton, (ed.), *The Red Screen*, London, 1992.

J. Leyda, *Kino*, London, 1983.

G. Roberts, *Forward Soviet!*, London, 1999.

R. Taylor, *The Politics of Soviet Cinema*, Cambridge, 1979.

R. Taylor and I. Christie in R. Taylor and I. Christie (eds), *The Film Factory*, London and Cambridge MA, 1988.

—— *Inside the Film Factory: New Approaches to Russian and Soviet Film*, London and New York, 1990.

D. J. Youngblood, *Soviet Cinema in the Silent Era*, Austin TX, 1991.

Documentary History, Practice and Theory

E. Barnouw, *Documentary. A History of Non-fiction Film*, Oxford, 1983.

B. Grant, and J. Sloniowski, (eds), *Documenting the Documentary*, Detroit, 1998.

J. Grierson, *Grierson on Documentary*, London, 1971.

G. Roy Levin, *Documentary Explorations*, New York, 1971.

B. Winston, *Claiming the Real*, London, 1995.

Russian/Soviet Cultural and Political History

S. Fitzpatrick, *The Russian Revolution 1928–1932*, London, 1978.

——, (ed.), *Cultural Revolution in Russia 1928–31*, London, 1978.

S. Fitzpatrick, A. Rabinovich and R. Stites, *Russia in the Era of N.E.P. Explorations in Soviet Society and Culture*, London, 1993.

G. Hosking, *A History of the Soviet Union*, London 1992.

M. McCauley, *Soviet Politics 1917–91*, London 1992.

R. Sakwa, *Soviet Politics*, London, 1989.

L. Shapiro, *The Communist Party of the Soviet Union*, London, 1973.

14· May 2001 Carts 17-95 (19-95), 8086C